New International Version

THE
GOLDEN TREASURY
OF
BIBLE WISDOM

Barbour Books
Westwood, New Jersey

© 1991 The LaMar Publishing Co.

Mass Market Edition ISBN 1-55748-223-3

Published by BARBOUR AND COMPANY, INC.,
P.O. Box 1219
Westwood, New Jersey

EVANGELICAL CHRISTIAN PUBLISHERS ASSOCIATION **ecpa** MEMBER

Typesetting by Typetronix, Inc., Cape Coral, Florida

Printed in the United States of America

DEDICATION

To the kind and courageous publishers and editors, in this and other lands, who have honored the God-given instrument of the printing press by publishing the best news of all, The Word of God, I dedicate this collection.

"The Lord announced the word, and great was the company of those who proclaimed it."

Psalm 68:11

Herschel B. Dean

This dedication was written by Herschel Dean prior to his untimely death February 9, 1986.

ACKNOWLEDGMENT

Since 1952, Rev. H. B. Dean's Bible verse and timely message columns have appeared daily in hundreds of newspapers throughout the United States and in other countries.

Printed under various titles, the works of Herschel Dean truly have been inspired Gospel seeds sown in the hearts of many thousands of readers, and have been cherished by people from all walks of life.

It is with prayerful gratitude for this servant of God's obedient and dedicated response to the inspiration of the Holy Spirit that we proudly present "THE GOLDEN TREASURY OF BIBLE WISDOM."

"God is not unjust; he will not forget your work and the love you have shown him . . ."
Hebrews 6:10

The LaMar Publishing Co.

Contents

Words of Assurance 9

The Bible 33

Faith 49

Family 67

Thoughts on Giving 77

God's Love 97

Words of Guidance 117

The Holy Spirit 139

Jesus, Lord and Saviour 153

Love 177

Obedience to God 189

Our Every Need 199

Peace — Happiness — Joy 223

Praising God 235

Prayer 253

Rebuking Satan 271

Salvation 279

Serving God 311

The Sovereignty of God 331

Spiritual Birth 343

Spiritual Neglect 353

Trusting God 363

Words of Warning 371

Miscellany 393

Words of
Assurance....

Words of Assurance

"And we know that in all things God works for the good of those who love him, who have been called according to his purpose."

Romans 8:28

If you are a believer in Christ, God has everything working for you, though at the moment it may seem to be going against you. Just because we can't see it is no sign that He is not doing it. "If God is for us, who can be against us?"

"For I am convinced that neither death nor life, neither angels nor demons, neither the present nor the future, nor any powers, neither height nor depth, nor anything else in all creation, will be able to separate us from the love of God that is in Christ Jesus our Lord."

Romans 8:38, 39

God is trying to get through with the news that you are a winner. Let Him!

" 'I have told you these things, so that in me you may have peace. In this world you will have trouble. But take heart! I have overcome the world.' "

John 16:33

What victory — and to think that we are a part of it. "As the Father has sent me, I am sending you." Christ in you, the hope of glory. Amen.

"I will bless those who bless you,
     and whoever curses you I will curse;
   and all peoples on earth
   will be blessed through you."

Genesis 12:3

What a sweeping promise! What an historical fact — and the end is not yet.

"But he said to me, 'My grace is sufficient for you, for my power is made perfect in weakness.' Therefore I will boast all the more gladly about my weaknesses, so that Christ's power may rest on me."

2 Corinthians 12:9

Just when you think it's all over, look for a breath of new life to pick you up. He is all sufficient and yours for the asking. ". . . I stand at the door and knock. If anyone hears my voice and opens the door, I will come in . . ."

" 'For God so loved the world that he gave his one and only Son, that whoever believes in him shall not perish but have eternal life.' "

John 3:16

If this was the only word we had from God, it would be enough. Put your name in the middle of it and get ready for excitement now and eternal life forever. Thanks, Father, You did it. We believe it.

" 'Come to me, all you who are weary and burdened, and I will give you rest.' "

Matthew 11:28

Here is the invitation to all for rest and reality, but we must take the initiative to realize it.

"He who dwells in the shelter of
the Most High
will rest in the shadow of the
Almighty."

Psalm 91:1

As we search for our place in life, may this be the first one that we find. Everything else will fall in line.

"Hezekiah received the letter from the messengers and read it. Then he went up to the temple of the Lord and spread it out before the Lord."
2 Kings 19:14

We should be as wise with the burdens of life! Take them before the Lord and leave them there, before they take us under. "He cares for you."

_____

"I will repay you for the years
    the locusts have eaten —
the great locust and the young
    locust,
the other locusts and the
    locust swarm —
    my great army that I sent among
      you."
Joel 2:25

If you feel like you have thrown your life to the wind, take a look at the only One who can make you a winner. He is the author of time and can make up for all that's lost. Take Jesus today and watch how quickly He can turn things around for you. Only God can take a life of wasted years and defeat and turn it all into victory. Let Him!

_____

" 'It is easier for heaven and earth to disappear than for the least stroke of a pen to drop out of the Law.' "

Luke 16:17

The Lord has never been known to go back on His Word or back down on His promises. "Only believe."

———————

"There remains, then, a Sabbath-rest for the people of God."

Hebrews 4:9

Only God's people can rest assured. "Come unto me, all you who are weary and burdened, and I will give you rest."

———————

"See, I have refined you, though not as silver; I have tested you in the furnace of affliction."

Isaiah 48:10

"No servant is greater than his master," and as Jesus was tested in the furnace of affliction and persecution, even so it is the furnace that refines us and makes us fit for real service. But always remember, "He knows how we are formed" and He is our strength in every trial.

———————

"Who shall separate us from the love of Christ?"

Romans 8:35

Many have tried to separate God's people from Him in various ways, but He says, "I will be with him in trouble." Men have hidden out in caves to read the Bible; they have been burned at the stake and thrown to the lions, but God has brought them through it all. "Our anchor holds."

––––––––––

"For I am with you, and no one is going to attack and harm you, because I have many people in this city."

Acts 18:10

In your darkest hour, remember that He who holds the whole world in the palm of His hand is watching and is able to deliver. "For he will command his angels to guard you in all your ways."

––––––––––

" 'They will be mine,' says the Lord Almighty, 'in the day when I make up my treasured possession. I will spare them, just as in compassion a man spares his son who serves him.' "

Malachi 3:17

God has His plans for His people, and through Christ, everyone can be a part of those plans.

———————

"For he will command his angels
concerning you
to guard you in all your ways."

Psalm 91:11

It's a dangerous thing to be on your own and away from God. Doubtless we would shudder and rejoice if we could see the Lord working behind the scenes of our lives keeping us from the many dangers that fall across our path.

———————

"Surely the arm of the Lord is not too short to save, nor his ear too dull to hear."

Isaiah 59:1

No matter how far down or how high up you are, the hand of God can reach you. No

one is out of reach. No one need be out of touch with the Lord.

———————

"His mother said to the servants, 'Do whatever he tells you.' "

John 2:5

You can proceed on His promise and move with confidence at His command. The miraculous is waiting for those who dare to take the Lord at His Word.

———————

"Again he prayed, and the heavens gave rain, and the earth produced its crops."

James 5:18

Here is the story of a man who, through faith and prayer, opened up Heaven. He is not in a class by himself. "And these signs will accompany those who believe . . ." Heaven will still open to those who approach it on the Lord's terms. "And I will do whatever you ask in my name . . ."

———————

"No temptation has seized you except what is common to man. And God is faithful; he will not let you be tempted beyond what you can bear. But when you are tempted, he will also provide a way out so that you can stand up under it."

1 Corinthians 10:13

Life is filled with a lot of subtle temptations that surrender only to the supernatural. "The Lord knows how to rescue godly men from trials . . ."

————————

"But will God really dwell on earth with men? . . ."

2 Chronicles 6:18

The greatest privilege of a Christian is that he enjoys the presence of the Lord now. "Never will I leave you; never will I forsake you."

————————

"If you make the Most High your
        dwelling —
even the Lord, who is my
        refuge —
then no harm will befall you,
no disaster will come near
        your tent."

Psalm 91:9, 10

Every believer has the right to claim this promise and live with confidence that God will keep His Word as we embrace the condition.

" 'Praise be to the Lord, who has given rest to his people Israel just as he promised. Not one word has failed of all the good promises he gave through his servant Moses.' "

1 Kings 8:56

Look at the record and leave the rest to Him. He will keep His Word with you. We are but to claim it.

"Commit your way to the Lord; trust in him and he will do this."

Psalm 37:5

God hears and remembers well. Simply turn it over to Him once, and see what happens.

" 'Don't be afraid,' the prophet answered. 'Those who are with us are more than those who are with them.'

"And Elisha prayed, 'O Lord, open his eyes so he may see.' Then the Lord opened the servant's eyes, and he looked and saw the hills full of horses and chariots of fire all around Elisha."

2 Kings 6:16, 17

Think miracles! God has everything under control. Keep your eyes on Him and not on the circumstances. "So do not fear, for I am with you . . ."

"As the rain and the snow
   come down from heaven,
 and do not return to it
   without watering the earth
 and making it bud and flourish,
   so that it yields seed for the
      sower and bread for the
      eater,
   so is my word that goes out
      from my mouth:
    It will not return to me empty,
   but will accomplish what I
      desire
 and achieve the purpose for
      which I sent it."

Isaiah 55:10, 11

Stay in there with the pure Word of God whoever you are and wherever you are. Whether you see it fulfilled the next day or in the next life, there is nothing but success and victory waiting for you. Father, thank You for Your faithful Word.

"The Spirit himself testifies with our spirit that we are God's children."

Romans 8:16

It's the harmony of our spirit and God's Spirit that bears testimony as to whether or not our hearts are right and we are His. If there is a trace of doubt, turn to Jesus now and clear it up while there is time.

" 'He is not here; he has risen, just as he said. Come and see the place where he lay.' "

Matthew 28:6

He is alive and at the right hand of the Father ever living to make intercession for us. "Because I live, you also will live." Thank You, Father, for the resurrection of Jesus, Your Son, and our assurance of eternal life through Him.

"Dear friend, I pray that you may enjoy good health and that all may go well with you, even as your soul is getting along well."

3 John 2

God wants us to believe for the best in all things, for He surely means for us to have them. "And I will do whatever you ask in my name."

"I desire to do your will, O my God . . ."

Psalm 40:8

Be willing for God to have His way and, though everything seems to go wrong, in the end you will see that God was right. "In all things God works for the good of those who love him, who have been called according to his purpose."

" 'Peace I leave with you; my peace I give you. I do not give to you as the world gives. Do not let your hearts be troubled and do not be afraid.' "

John 14:27

About all the world has to offer is temporary tranquilizers in one form or another to keep the mind off the condition of the heart. Trust Christ for real peace of mind and heart.

———————————

" 'Be still, and know that I am
    God;
I will be exalted among the
    nations,
I will be exalted in the earth.' "

Psalm 46:10

In an age of haste, it is good to remember that there is yet a lot to be learned and accomplished in the art of just waiting. Wait on the Lord and He shall renew thy strength.

———————————

"The Lord is my light and my salvation — whom shall I fear? The Lord is the stronghold of my life — of whom shall I be afraid?"

Psalm 27:1

The man who walks with God doesn't have to run from anything. "So do not fear, for I am with you . . ."

———————————

". . . 'Death has been swallowed up in victory.'

" 'Where, O death, is your victory?
Where, O death, is your sting?' "

1 Corinthians 15:54, 55

Death is not a dead end but a doorway. Jesus said, "He who believes in me will live, even though he dies."

———————————

"And we know that in all things God works for the good of those who love him, who have been called according to his purpose."

Romans 8:28

God has a way of making things come out right for those who love Him and serve Him. "No good thing does he withhold from those whose walk is blameless."

———————————

"You, dear children, are from God and have overcome them, because the one who is in you is greater than the one who is in the world."

1 John 4:4

We come to master the problems from without when we learn to appropriate power from within. "Nothing will be impossible for you."

———————————

"No temptation has seized you except what is common to man. And God is faithful; he will not let you be tempted beyond what you can bear. But when you are tempted, he will also provide a way out so that you can stand up under it."

1 Corinthians 10:13

God walks in the midst of all the trials of His children with outstretched hands of answers and assurance. He is our Guide who knows the way out; you can trust Him.

———————

"There remains, then, a Sabbath-rest for the people of God."

Hebrews 4:9

Only the people of God can rest assured.

———————

"He said, 'Look! I see four men walking around in the fire, unbound and unharmed, and the fourth looks like a son of the gods.' "

Daniel 3:25

In every fiery trial of life, the child of God can expect the presence of the Saviour to see him through.

———————

"You will not fear the terror of the night, nor the arrow that flies by day."

Psalm 91:5

Our gracious Lord has provided for our protection, as well as our pardon. "Don't be afraid; just believe."

———————————

"Blessed is the nation whose God is the Lord . . ."

Psalm 33:12

If God is in the government, faith will be in the people. A nation under God will never be under another power.

———————————

"What, then, shall we say in response to this? If God is for us, who can be against us?"

Romans 8:31

God with us is not always a good sign that man is for us, but ". . . the one who is in you is greater than the one who is in the world."

———————————

"Blessed is he whose help is the God of Jacob, whose hope is in the Lord his God."

Psalm 146:5

If you have the Lord on your side, the world can stand on its head and you can still remain calm.

––––––––––

"I write these things to you who believe in the name of the Son of God so that you may know that you have eternal life."

1 John 5:13

Salvation through Christ carries with it a guaranteed future in Heaven and a wonderful life while on earth.

––––––––––

"If you make the Most High your dwelling — even the Lord, who is my refuge — then no harm will befall you, no disaster will come near your tent."

Psalm 91:9, 10

Living with God, and for Him, has a lot of built-in benefits that we can't afford to be without. "My Presence will go with you . . ." "If God is for us, who can be against us?"

––––––––––

"A righteous man may have many troubles, but the Lord delivers him from them all."

Psalm 34:19

The people of God are not immune to problems, but escorted through them. "If God is for us, who can be against us?" "I am with you." Thanks, Lord!

———————————

"I can do everything through him who gives me strength."

Philippians 4:13

Get a picture of Christ in you and develop it by reading and believing this promise. You are in for some living that will surprise you.

———————————

"I have set the Lord always before me. Because he is at my right hand, I will not be shaken."

Psalm 16:8

No matter how things look, keep your eyes on the Lord. He can bring miracles out of mistakes.

———————————

"You are my hiding place; you will protect me from trouble and surround me with songs of deliverance.   *Selah*"

Psalm 32:7

Everything we need, He is. God forgive us for our failure to see this truth. You will never relive today. Make it a good one with God's help.

———————

"I will lie down and sleep in peace, for you alone, O Lord, make me dwell in safety."

Psalm 4:8

Rest assured, God is wide awake. "The angel of the Lord encamps around those who fear him . . ."

———————

"So we say with confidence, 'The Lord is my helper; I will not be afraid. What can man do to me?' "

Hebrews 13:6

When you think of what you have going for you, how can you let anything get you down? "Fear not, I am with you" — Jesus!

———————

" 'In the last days, God says, I will pour out my Spirit on all people. Your sons and daughters will prophesy, your young men will see visions, your old men will dream dreams. Even on my servants, both men and women, I will pour out my Spirit in those days, and they will prophesy.' "

Acts 2:17, 18

We are living in the midst of these days and the demonstration of God's mighty power around the world is ample proof. "The promise is for you . . ."

" 'I will surely gather them from all the lands where I banish them in my furious anger and great wrath; I will bring them back to this place and let them live in safety. I will give them singleness of heart and action, so that they will always fear me for their own good and the good of their children after them.' "

Jeremiah 32:37, 39

He will keep His Word! He has kept His Word! "Heaven and earth will pass away, but my words will never pass away."

" '*Abba*, Father,' he said, 'everything is possible for you. Take this cup from me. Yet not what I will, but what you will.' "

Mark 14:36

We sometimes fear the will of God as though He has forgotten something. He is mindful, merciful and has never made a mistake and is working all things out for our good and His glory. We praise Thee, O God.

––––––––––

"He will bless those who fear the Lord — small and great alike. May the Lord make you increase, both you and your children."

Psalm 115:13, 14

What a promise! Claim it! The Lord is not slack concerning His promise. "Heaven and earth will pass away, but my words will never pass away."

––––––––––

" 'And if I go and prepare a place for you, I will come back and take you to be with me that you also may be where I am. You know the way to the place where I am going.' "

John 14:3

Don't get too earthbound! This good Word from the Lord, Himself, makes it clear that He is coming again to receive those for whom He has prepared a wonderful place. Now to make sure you are going to make it, simply acknowledge your need and invite Him to come into your heart. ". . . whoever comes to me I will never drive away."

———————

"Remember me for this, O my God, and do not blot out what I have so faithfully done for the house of my God and its services."

Nehemiah 13:14

The Lord has a long memory and many rewards for the faithful. Stay in there with the work of God and the servant of God. "[He] will certainly not lose his reward."

———————

The Bible....

The Bible

"Your word is a lamp to my feet and a light for my path."

Psalm 119:105

The Word of the Lord was meant to be used by men in travel from earth to Heaven. Perhaps the reason we have run into so many dark and gloomy roads along the way is because we have not recognized it.

———————

"The Lord continued to appear at Shiloh, and there he revealed himself to Samuel through his word."

1 Samuel 3:21

The Bible is God's way of revealing Himself. "Faith comes from hearing the message, and the message is heard through the word of Christ." Build your faith. Spend more time in your Father's book.

———————

"Jesus answered, 'It is written: "Man does not live on bread alone." ' "

Luke 4:4

Man needs something more than the products of his own hands in this life and in the life to come.

———————

"The grass withers and the flowers fall, but the word of our God stands forever."

Isaiah 40:8

Long after the Bible's critics are dead and buried, the Word of God will still be standing. "Thy word is truth."

" 'It is easier for heaven and earth to disappear than for the least stroke of a pen to drop out of the Law.' "

Luke 16:17

The Word of God has buried its critics and still marches on as conqueror and comforter, spreading its light to the darkest corners of the earth. "Your word is truth."

"But the word of God continued to increase and spread."

Acts 12:24

This has been the history of the Word of God and this is its future. The truly wise will keep on sharing it faithfully and quickly. "My word . . . will not return to me empty."

"And he said to them: 'You have a fine way of setting aside the commands of God in order to observe your own traditions! . . . Thus you nullify the word of God by your tradition that you have handed down. And you do many things like that.' "

Mark 7:9, 13

A lot of people are still trying to pass off their "good old tradition" for the Old Time Gospel. It wouldn't work then, nor will it work now. "Diligently study the Scriptures . . ."

―――――――――

"But you, Bethlehem Ephrathah, though you are small among the clans of Judah, out of you will come for me one who will be ruler over Israel, whose origins are from of old, from ancient times."

Micah 5:2

The amazing accuracy of prophecy already fulfilled should make us avid readers of the Bible . . . God's timepiece of what is yet to be.

―――――――――

"Always learning but never able to acknowledge the truth."

2 Timothy 3:7

One of the great tragedies of our time is that most of it is spent in learning error and dodging truth. "Your word is truth."

"Take the helmet of salvation and the sword of the Spirit, which is the word of God."

Ephesians 6:17

We are to take God's Word to heart, while holding it forth as the world's only hope. Have you read the Bible today — have you shared it with someone? "My words will never pass away."

"What you heard from me, keep as the pattern of sound teaching, with faith and love in Christ Jesus."

2 Timothy 1:13

We should keep the Gospel simple, not mystic, and be careful to speak to the present need. There is a danger of belaboring the Scripture instead of just delivering it. "Heaven and earth will pass away, but my words will never pass away."

"Jesus answered, 'It is written: "Man does not live on bread alone." ' "

Luke 4:4

A life dependent only on the physical and material is in for some lean times . . . but if the Spiritual intake of His Word has equal time with the physical, we can count on some strong bodies and great Christians.

"There is a way that seems right to a man, but in the end it leads to death."

Proverbs 14:12

Don't look at the way you feel, but to the Word of God. "Your word is a lamp to my feet and a light for my path."

"He who scorns instruction will pay for it, but he who respects a command is rewarded."

Proverbs 13:13

God is watching our reaction to His Word. Have you heard or read any of it lately? Our reward or rebuke is based on how we regard it.

" 'Heaven and earth will pass away, but my words will never pass away.' "

Mark 13:31

Long after man has had his say, the Word of God will still be standing. In view of this, we ought to spend more time with it.

────────────

"Your word, O Lord, is eternal; it stands firm in the heavens."

Psalm 119:89

The Word of God has been proofread in Heaven, and its promises are ready for everyone on earth. Read and believe. He will not go back on His Word.

────────────

"For prophecy never had its origin in the will of man, but men spoke from God as they were carried along by the Holy Spirit."

2 Peter 1:21

When you read the Bible, remember this. Here is the reason it is so powerful and lasting. "My words will never pass away . . . My word . . . will not return to me empty."

────────────

" 'If anyone chooses to do God's will, he will find out whether my teaching comes from God or whether I speak on my own.' "

John 7:17

The Bible has stood the test of time and talents, and it still marches on bringing release and peace to all who will obey its instructions. "Heaven and earth will pass away, but my words will never pass away."

———————

"I have hidden your word in my heart that I might not sin against you."

Psalm 119:11

Take His Word to heart. It points the way to the abundant life and eternal life.

———————

". . . Great is the Lord's anger that burns against us because our fathers have not obeyed the words of this book; they have not acted in accordance with all that is written there concerning us."

2 Kings 22:13

Every generation will rise and answer for its neglect of the "Book of Books."

———————

" 'And the gospel must first be preached to all nations.' "

Mark 13:10

The Gospel is the only guide capable of leading the world out of the darkness and into the marvelous light of Christ. "It is the power of God for the salvation of everyone who believes . . ."

———————

" '. . . your word is truth.' "

John 17:17

Trust the word of man and you get what man can do. Trust the Word of God and you get what God has promised. He is able to do the exceeding and the abundant above all that we can ask or think.

———————

"Do your best to present yourself to God as one approved, a workman who does not need to be ashamed and who correctly handles the word of truth."

2 Timothy 2:15

A person should not only study the Bible for what they can get out of it, but for what it can get out of them.

———————

"Be very strong; be careful to obey all that is written in the Book of the Law of Moses, without turning aside to the right or to the left."

Joshua 23:6

More time with the greatest book on earth will mean better times for all of us. Jesus said, "Heaven and earth will pass away, but my words will never pass away."

———————————

" 'The days are coming,' declares the Sovereign Lord, 'when I will send a famine through the land — not a famine of food or a thirst for water, but a famine of hearing the words of the Lord. Men will stagger from sea to sea and wander from north to east, searching for the word of the Lord, but they will not find it.' "

Amos 8:11, 12

God has given a gift and left a gift — His Son and His Word. Treat it with reverence, read it with diligence. Some day it will be scarce and man will be hungry for it.

———————————

"So do not be ashamed to testify about our Lord, or ashamed of me his prisoner. But join with me in suffering for the gospel, by the power of God."

2 Timothy 1:8

People who are bent on taking the Bible out of public life would be just as happy if they didn't have to face it from the pulpit. Jesus said, "If anyone is ashamed of me and my words . . . the Son of Man will be ashamed of him when he comes in his Father's glory with the holy angels."

"Your word, O Lord, is eternal; it stands firm in the heavens."

Psalm 119:89

His Word is everlasting and never failing. We ought to give more heed to it.

"I seek you with all my heart; do not let me stray from your commands."

Psalm 119:10

The Bible is a map to peace, happiness, and Heaven. Follow it and you will have a safe journey. Wander from it and you are in trouble. Discover God in His Word.

"Consequently, faith comes from hearing the message, and the message is heard through the word of Christ."

Romans 10:17

People who want to have more faith ought to be more faithful in reading the Word of God. "Your word is a lamp to my feet and a light for my path."

"That night the king could not sleep; so he ordered the book of the chronicles, the record of his reign, to be brought in and read to him."

Esther 6:1

The reading of the Old Book will still settle a lot of nerves and point humanity to a land where strife and tears are strangers.

"He who scorns instruction will pay for it, but he who respects a command is rewarded."

Proverbs 13:13

Respect His Word. Someday you will be judged by it. Use it today as a release of God's power. "The words I have spoken to you are spirit and they are life."

"For prophecy never had its origin in the will of man, but men spoke from God as they were carried along by the Holy Spirit."

2 Peter 1:21

The inspired Word inspires us. That's why we should spend more time with it. Make Bible reading a must. "Faith comes from hearing the message, and the message is heard through the word of Christ."

"Blessed is the one who reads the words of this prophecy, and blessed are those who hear it and take to heart what is written in it, because the time is near."

Revelation 1:3

This is another admonition to read God's Word. If we only knew the benefits of the Bible, nothing could keep us from it. "Your word is truth."

"In God, whose word I praise, in the Lord, whose word I praise —"

Psalm 56:10

One of the great failures of our time is that we have put too much emphasis on man's word and too little emphasis on the Word of God. "The word of the Lord stands forever."

———————

"Jesus answered, 'It is written: "Man does not live on bread alone, but on every word that comes from the mouth of God." ' "

Matthew 4:4

No wonder life gets to be so dull with just a steady diet of what the world has to offer. Build up your faith, brighten up your living. Read a portion of the Word of God daily.

———————

"Consequently, faith comes from hearing the message, and the message is heard through the word of Christ."

Romans 10:17

To increase your faith, increase your intake of the Word by hearing, reading and praying it. Dear Holy Spirit, read the Word of God through us and help us to retain It in our hearts for the glory of God and in Jesus' name. Amen.

―――――――――

" 'Heaven and earth will pass away, but my words will never pass away.' "

Matthew 24:35

The Word of God is going to stand. Shouldn't we spend more time with It? "The word of the Lord stands forever."

―――――――――

"Then those who feared the Lord talked with each other, and the Lord listened and heard. A scroll of remembrance was written in his presence concerning those who feared the Lord and honored his name. 'They will be mine,' says the Lord Almighty, 'in the day when I make up my treasured possession. I will spare them, just as in compassion a man spares his son who serves him.' "

Malachi 3:16, 17

Here is a unique and beautiful bond between believers that should be marked by constant fellowship. To neglect it is an invitation to some lean times in our spiritual lives that are often hard to recover.

―――――――――

"Carefully follow the terms of this covenant, so that you may prosper in everything you do."

Deuteronomy 29:9

Far from being a dry book, the Bible is a guide to all that we have dreamed of. Read a little of it every day and long after you have read, it will be back to bless you. "I have hidden your word in my heart that I might not sin against you."

Faith....

Faith

". . . This is the victory that has overcome the world, even our faith."

1 John 5:4

Overcoming faith! That is the need of the hour. Not only faith to start on, but faith to stand on. Faith that is good enough to live by is good enough to die by. "Lord . . . increase our faith!"

"The Lord's hand was with them, and a great number of people believed and turned to the Lord."

Acts 11:21

In order to have His hand with you, it is absolutely necessary to leave all in His hand. When God is with us, people will believe, and when they believe, they will turn to the Lord. "Let the beauty of Jesus be seen in me."

"Even though I walk through the valley of the shadow of death, I will fear no evil, for you are with me; your rod and your staff, they comfort me."

Psalm 23:4

The man who has put his faith in God will not be afraid of the future. "Have faith in God."

" 'Everything is possible for him who believes.' "

Mark 9:23

Daring Christians are a delight to the Lord.

" '. . . not my will, but yours be done.' "

Luke 22:42

God knows best and He will do what is best. He is our advocate; trust His judgment. "Without faith it is impossible to please God."

". . . a man came along who was covered with leprosy. When he saw Jesus, he fell with his face to the ground and begged him, 'Lord, if you are willing, you can make me clean.' Jesus reached out his hand and touched the man. 'I am willing,' he said. 'Be clean!' And immediately the leprosy left him."

Luke 5:12, 13

With the acknowledgement that something was wrong came the assurance that there was One who could make it right. "I am willing . . . Be clean!"

"He looked around at them all, and then said to the man, 'Stretch out your hand.' He did so, and his hand was completely restored."

Luke 6:10

Blessed is the man who obeys the voice of Jesus and believes Him for the inexplainable and the impossible. Believe only. "He is able."

"And without faith it is impossible to please God, because anyone who comes to him must believe that he exists and that he rewards those who earnestly seek him."

Hebrews 11:6

Faith takes the strain out of life and the suspense out of eternity. God give us faith to remove mountains and grace to look over the little hills.

"Simon answered, 'Master, we've worked hard all night and haven't caught anything. But because you say so, I will let down the nets.' When they had done so, they caught such a large number of fish that their nets began to break.'"

Luke 5:5, 6

Jesus didn't go to where the fish were necessarily, but to where the faith was. He will honor our faith and obedience.

"When Jesus saw their faith, he said to the paralytic, 'Son, your sins are forgiven.' "

Mark 2:5

Apparently God honors the faith of the believer in the behalf of those who have none. A religion of ritual and works can wear you out. A faith that believes God for anything can lift you up. "Without faith it is impossible to please God."

" 'Lord, if it's you,' Peter replied, 'tell me to come to you on the water.' 'Come,' he said. Then Peter got down out of the boat, walked on the water and came toward Jesus. . . ."

Matthew 14:28, 29

When we step out on faith, the Lord will give us something to stand on. "This is the victory that has overcome the world, even our faith." "Only believe."

"And my God will meet all your needs according to his glorious riches in Christ Jesus."

Philippians 4:19

He supplies what we believe Him for; not what we wish for. Have faith in God. He is able.

" 'So I say to you: Ask and it will be given to you; seek and you will find; knock and the door will be opened to you.' "

Luke 11:9

Here is a formula that puts our faith to work in getting what we need and what He wants us to have. Pray on! Believe only!

" 'If you believe, you will receive whatever you ask for in prayer.' "

Matthew 21:22

Go for a miracle. "Everything is possible for him who believes." Lord, we believe!

"Then the father realized that this was the exact time at which Jesus had said to him, 'Your son will live.' So he and all his household believed."

John 4:53

The Lord needs to only say the word and wonders appear. He has spoken. Let us believe what He said . . . and is saying to us now. "Believe only."

" 'If you remain in me and my words remain in you, ask whatever you wish, and it will be given you.' "

John 15:7

This does not call for a constant "tug of war" striving and struggling, but a simple natural trust as we release our faith to the Father in the name of Jesus. In so doing, we appropriate what He has already provided. Praise His name for it!

"In the same way, faith by itself, if it is not accompanied by action, is dead."

James 2:17

Faith becomes effective when it becomes active. Take it out of the talking and thinking stage and put it to work practically, quickly and prayerfully. ". . . in accordance with the measure of faith God has given you." It is enough . . . use it!

———————

"When evening came, many who were demon-possessed were brought to him, and he drove out the spirits with a word and healed all the sick. This was to fulfill what was spoken through the prophet Isaiah:

'He took up our infirmities and carried our diseases.' "

Matthew 8:16, 17

The ministry of Jesus was one of action and authority. He has passed on to all believers that same boldness if we will but see it and use it. He said, "Anyone who has faith in me will do what I have been doing. He will do even greater things than these . . ."

———————

" 'I tell you the truth, if anyone says to this mountain, "Go, throw yourself into the sea," and does not doubt in his heart but believes that what he says will happen, it will be done for him.' "

Mark 11:23

Do what Jesus said. Speak to your mountains. They have done the talking long enough. "For nothing is impossible with God."

"This is the confidence we have in approaching God: that if we ask anything according to his will, he hears us. And if we know that he hears us — whatever we ask — we know that we have what we asked of him."

1 John 5:14, 15

Many find things in His Word and start wondering if it's for them. Don't be looking for conditions but compassion. Take Him at His Word. He has "exalted above all things [his] name and [his] word."

"I tell you the truth, anyone who has faith in me will do what I have been doing. He will do even greater things than these, because I am going to the Father. And I will do whatever you ask in my name, so that the Son may bring glory to the Father. You may ask me for anything in my name, and I will do it."

John 14:12-14

Release your faith with me as we look to the Father. Jesus, I take You at Your Word and believe now that multitudes will be saved, believers filled with the Holy Spirit, others healed, and needs met in every part of their lives in Your Name and for the glory of God, Amen.

"Then Caleb silenced the people before Moses and said, 'We should go up and take possession of the land, for we can certainly do it.' "

Numbers 13:30

Don't you like to hear someone who follows a negative report with some straight forward talk expressing a God-given faith? You be that person. Believe God for anything. Speak your faith and He will surely come through.

"He replied, 'If you have faith as small as a mustard seed, you can say to this mulberry tree, "Be uprooted and planted in the sea," and it will obey you.' "

Luke 17:6

Spoken faith is a mighty force capable of bringing to pass what appears to be the impossible. Dare to believe God for anything. Father, we believe You for great miracles in Jesus' name. Amen.

"By faith the walls of Jericho fell, after the people had marched around them for seven days."

Hebrews 11:30

There is no wall thick enough or armed enough to stand against one seed of faith. On with the march. Faith, praise, power and obedience will see the walls down and the windows of Heaven open. Praise God!

"And they asked each other, 'Who will roll the stone away from the entrance of the tomb?' But when they looked up, they saw that the stone, which was very large, had been rolled away."

Mark 16:3, 4

Like us, we anticipate blockades that have long since been removed. Get rid of that negative thinking and nothing shall be impossible unto you. "Believe only."

"He replied, 'Because you have so little faith. I tell you the truth, if you have faith as small as a mustard seed, you can say to this mountain, "Move from here to there" and it will move. Nothing will be impossible for you.' "

Matthew 17:20

Take another look at this and never again make little of your faith, no matter how small it may look to you. It is mountain moving. Use it and a miracle is in the making.

"He said to his disciples, 'Why are you so afraid? Do you still have no faith?' "

Mark 4:40

God must stand amazed at our lack of belief in a world of miracles.

———————

" 'You may ask me for anything in my name, and I will do it.' "

John 14:14

Answered prayer yields to the bold approach and daring faith. "Everything is possible for him who believes." "He is able."

———————

" 'For nothing is impossible with God.' "

Luke 1:37

What the world needs is more mustard seed faith to remove man-made mountains. "According to your faith will it be done to you."

———————

"The Lord will watch over your coming and going both now and forevermore."

Psalm 121:8

Our gracious Father gives direction and protection to those who follow in faith. "I am with you."

———————

"Taking him by the right hand, he helped him up, and instantly the man's feet and ankles became strong. He jumped to his feet and began to walk. Then he went with them into the temple courts, walking and jumping, and praising God."

Acts 3:7, 8

If our faith is up-to-date, you can be sure that the days of miracles are not past. "I the Lord do not change."

"So do not throw away your confidence; it will be richly rewarded."

Hebrews 10:35

If you have earnestly prayed about it and have the conviction that what you are doing is right, the Lord will furnish the courage to see you through. "Only believe."

". . . the God we serve is able. . . ."

Daniel 3:17

There is no limit to what the Lord will do in answer to daring faith. "For nothing is impossible with God."

"And without faith it is impossible to please God, because anyone who comes to him must believe that he exists and that he rewards those who earnestly seek him."

Hebrews 11:6

The man who truly walks by faith will not run the risk of being embarrassed. "Have faith in God."

"Even though I walk through the valley of the shadow of death, I will fear no evil, for you are with me; your rod and your staff, they comfort me."

Psalm 23:4

The man who has put his faith in God will not be afraid of the future. "Have faith in God."

"Jesus said to the woman, 'Your faith has saved you; go in peace.' "

Luke 7:50

Put up whatever faith you have and He will match it. Then look for miracles. God has given every man a measure of faith. Use it!

"Say to those with fearful hearts, 'Be strong, do not fear; your God will come, he will come with vengeance; with divine retribution he will come to save you.' "

Isaiah 35:4

When fear comes calling, turn up the volume of your faith. "So do not fear, for I am with you ... I will uphold you with my righteous right hand."

"For by the grace given me I say to every one of you: Do not think of yourself more highly than you ought, but rather think of yourself with sober judgment, in accordance with the measure of faith God has given you."

Romans 12:3

Don't pray for more faith. Use what you have and watch it multiply. "According to your faith will it be done to you."

"For God did not give us a spirit of timidity, but a spirit of power, of love and of self-discipline."

2 Timothy 1:7

Turn your fears back with your faith. "God did not give us a spirit of timidity," but He has given us a measure of faith. It is enough.

It is mountain moving. "Your faith has made thee whole." "Praise God from whom all blessings flow."

"By faith Abraham, when called to go to a place he would later receive as his inheritance, obeyed and went, even though he did not know where he was going."

Hebrews 11:8

If we take the first step of faith, it won't be too long until we see that we are not alone. "I will never leave thee nor forsake thee." The big word is obey. The big fact is that He loves us and has plans for our lives.

Family....

Family

" 'If you return to the Lord, then your brothers and your children will be shown compassion by their captors and will come back to this land, for the Lord your God is gracious and compassionate. He will not turn his face from you if you return to him.' "

2 Chronicles 30:9

As a nation, family, church, or individual, so much depends on the direction we take. Start here — "As for me and my household, we will serve the Lord."

———————

" 'How can I go back to my father if the boy is not with me? . . .' "

Genesis 44:34

In our great anxiety to see that our children won't miss anything, we should be super-careful that they don't miss the spiritual. Lead them to God, and take them to church. Forever you will be glad.

———————

" '. . . Didn't I tell you not to sin against the boy?' "

Genesis 42:22

To deprive a child of a Christian home and Christian training is to sin against the child. Failure to convert them and failure to love them is to sin against them. Do not fail to consider the child, lest you find yourself fighting against God and His will.

———————

"But Samuel was ministering before the Lord — a boy wearing a linen ephod."

1 Samuel 2:18

It doesn't take a grown person to do things for the Lord. He has been able to accomplish a lot more in the lives of many children than in the lives of their parents. "A little child shall lead them."

———————

"Children, obey your parents in everything, for this pleases the Lord."

Colossians 3:20

The strained relationship between children and parents can usually be traced to the child's disregard of what the parents have to say and the parents disregard of what God has to say. For a better home life, make it Christ centered.

———————

"Train a child in the way he should go, and when he is old he will not turn from it."

Proverbs 22:6

Some parents seem bent on giving a child everything but a Christian home. Lead your child to Christ. Take your child to church!

———————

"(If anyone does not know how to manage his own family, how can he take care of God's church?)"

1 Timothy 3:5

The man who would assume some authority in God's house ought to be thoroughly Christian in his own house.

———————

"There are those who curse their fathers and do not bless their mothers."

Proverbs 30:11

Children who disrespect a good mother and father automatically incur the displeasure of Almighty God.

———————

"Near the cross of Jesus stood his mother . . ."

John 19:25

"Mother's prayers have followed you!" If she is still with you and you can't see her in person, whatever it costs, call and express your love to her. I wish I had the privilege.

"Do not wear yourself out to get rich; have the wisdom to show restraint. Cast but a glance at riches, and they are gone, for they will surely sprout wings and fly off to the sky like an eagle."

Proverbs 23:4, 5

Before one of you has to leave the other, wouldn't it be wise to invest in that which will always be? If it's all tied up, now is the time to let it loose in the work of the Lord. "Seek first his kingdom . . ."

" 'A man's enemies will be the members of his own household.' "

Matthew 10:36

Since God deals with people individually, don't be discouraged if even your family is without understanding as to what He is telling you — nor be deterred by what they think or say.

" 'I prayed for this child, and the Lord has granted me what I asked of him. So now I give him to the Lord. For his whole life he will be given over to the Lord.' "

1 Samuel 1:27, 28

Dedicating a child to God is of even more importance than educating him.

———————————

"These commandments that I give you today are to be upon your hearts. Impress them on your children. Talk about them when you sit at home and when you walk along the road, when you lie down and when you get up."

Deuteronomy 6:6, 7

Do you wonder what is wrong with our children today? We have gotten away from instructing them in God's laws. More of the Word of God should be rehearsed and taught in the home.

———————————

"They replied, 'Believe in the Lord Jesus, and you will be saved — you and your household.' "

Acts 16:31

Pray on! Believe for the whole house. Father, I join with them in believing for their

whole family. Save them by Thy grace, in Jesus' name. Amen.

" 'As for your children that you said would be taken as plunder, I will bring them in to enjoy the land you have rejected.' "

Numbers 14:31

It is so often the case that God can do more with the children than He can with their parents. "Unless you change and become like little children, you will never enter the kingdom of heaven."

"They replied, 'Believe in the Lord Jesus, and you will be saved — you and your household.' "

Acts 16:31

Take this good word home with you, and ask God to honor it. I will believe with you. Father, on the basis of Your Word which says that "If two of you on earth agree about anything you ask for, it will be done for you by my Father in heaven." I believe with them for the salvation of their family and for any other need that they may have. In Jesus' name, Amen and thank You.

"All your sons will be taught by the Lord, and great will be your children's peace."

Isaiah 54:13

Get the child to God and to the Lord's house while there is time. You can be sure that the enemy of all that is good and wholesome will be after them. Don't squander the privilege to worship. Millions before and multitudes now would love the opportunity.

"Train a child in the way he should go, and when he is old he will not turn from it."

Proverbs 22:6

Get as much good going as you can quickly! Set some standards; emphasize the spiritual; give the Word of God and the church a place of prominence; and let love be in evidence in the home. God will honor it.

"The wise woman builds her house, but with her own hands the foolish one tears hers down."

Proverbs 14:1

Look who is regarded as a great home builder. The good atmosphere that a wife and mother creates around the home is priceless and everlasting. "Mother's prayers have followed you."

Thoughts on Giving....

Thoughts on Giving

" 'Give, and it will be given to you. A good measure, pressed down, shaken together and running over, will be poured into your lap. For with the measure you use, it will be measured to you.' "

Luke 6:38

A man's security is not in his savings, but in his giving. The Lord loves a cheerful giver.

"If a king judges the poor with fairness, his throne will always be secure."

Proverbs 29:14

The ministry to the poor lives on forever as one of the greatest tests of sincerity of the human being. "Whatever you did for one of the least of these brothers of mine, you did for me."

"Any who had precious stones gave them to the treasury of the temple of the Lord . . ."

1 Chronicles 29:8

Giving God the leftovers didn't originate with Old Testament giving habits. If they tithed before Christ came, surely we should at least do as much. Quit tipping God and start tithing. "God loves a cheerful giver."

"So Moses went back to the Lord and said, 'Oh, what a great sin these people have committed! They have made themselves gods of gold.' "

Exodus 32:31

Humanity has ever been the same. Gold is to be a servant. It is when we elevate it to a god that we are in serious trouble. "The love of money is a root of all kinds of evil." If you have means, make them count for the Master.

"But God said to him, 'You fool! This very night your life will be demanded from you. Then who will get what you have prepared for yourself?' "

Luke 12:20

People who busy themselves by laying up earthly treasure are apt to discover that it has cost them Heaven. Men ought to use their means in the spread of the Gospel, in the winning of the lost.

" 'Bring the whole tithe into the storehouse, that there may be food in my house. Test me in this,' says the Lord Almighty, 'and see if I will not throw open the floodgates of heaven and pour out so much blessing that you will not have room enough for it.' "

Malachi 3:10

Ten percent of our income belongs to God and He has ways of seeing that we pay it. "Give, and it will be given to you . . ."

" 'For whoever wants to save his life will lose it, but whoever loses his life for me will save it.' "

Luke 9:24

Live miserly with your life and your means and, no matter what you have in the end, you will die a poor failure.

" 'A tithe of everything from the land, whether grain from the soil or fruit from the trees, belongs to the Lord; it is holy to the Lord.' "

Leviticus 27:30

Is ten percent of what He has given you too much to ask for the work that you claim, as a Christian, to be the most important thing on earth? Try tithing for one month and see the miracle of it all.

———————————

" 'Heal the sick, raise the dead, cleanse those who have leprosy, drive out demons. Freely you have received, freely give.' "

Matthew 10:8

Learn to be generous with what God has given you. You can't outgive the Lord. "Give, and it will be given to you."

———————————

"Cast your bread upon the waters, for after many days you will find it again."

Ecclesiastes 11:1

Forget about knowing the results and attend to the sowing. You will be surprised some day at the power of the Gospel seed you have planted. "My word . . . will not return to me empty."

———————————

"Calling his disciples to him, Jesus said, 'I tell you the truth, this poor widow has put more into the treasury than all the others.'"

Mark 12:43

This has always been true on the average. The poor people support the work of God, while the wealthy give a few crumbs for the cause of Christ while off in search of some project to exalt their own name above His. Why don't you call your pastor and ask what you can do to really make your means count?

"If anyone has material possessions and sees his brother in need but has no pity on him, how can the love of God be in him?"

1 John 3:17

Here is a question that can only be answered by action. Today, God will use you to help someone in need. See to it that you obey His voice. "Whatever you did for one of the least of these brothers of mine, you did for me."

"Do not withhold good from those who deserve it, when it is in your power to act. Do not say to your neighbor, 'Come back later; I'll give it tomorrow' — when you now have it with you."

Proverbs 3:27, 28

We can get so busy talking spiritual that we neglect to do something practical! The Church could use more Christians in work clothes. Share with some needy person today.

———————

"On the first day of every week, each one of you should set aside a sum of money in keeping with his income, saving it up, so that when I come no collections will have to be made."

1 Corinthians 16:2

The Bible calls for the support of the Church and the cause of Christ by systematic giving, persistent praying, and dedicated sharing by those who claim an experience with the Lord.

———————

". . . 'What is it, Lord?' he asked. The angel answered, 'Your prayers and gifts to the poor have come up as a memorial offering before God.' "

Acts 10:4

Man's greatest strength is in his straight line to Heaven. Keep it busy. The whole bounty of God is waiting to be delivered.

———————

"And this stone that I have set up as a pillar will be God's house, and of all that you give me I will give you a tenth."

Genesis 28:22

The faith of every believer ought to be shared by systematic giving and some supernatural living. The more you give, the more you will want to give, and the more you will have to give.

———————

"Blessed is he who has regard for the weak; the Lord delivers him in times of trouble. The Lord will protect him and preserve his life; he will bless him in the land and not surrender him to the desire of his foes."

Psalm 41:1, 2

Being good to the poor carries with it a powerful promise. Who wouldn't want to have a part in it? "Be kind."

" 'For I was hungry and you gave me nothing to eat, I was thirsty and you gave me nothing to drink, I was a stranger and you did not invite me in, I needed clothes and you did not clothe me, I was sick and in prison and you did not look after me.' "

Matthew 25:42, 43

Jesus often appears in the form of neglected and little people, to see if we will do even the simple things as proof of our love and loyalty to Him personally.

"Amaziah asked the man of God, 'But what about the hundred talents I paid for these Israelite troops?' The man of God replied, 'The Lord can give you much more than that.' "

2 Chronicles 25:9

You will never be able to top God in giving, no matter what it is. "Give, and it will be given to you . . ."

" 'You are under a curse — the whole nation of you — because you are robbing me. Bring the whole tithe into the storehouse, that there may be food in my house. Test me in this,' says the Lord Almighty, 'and see if I will not throw open the floodgates of heaven and pour out so much blessing that you will not have room enough for it.' "

Malachi 3:9, 10

Give yourself out of that predicament! "Honor the Lord with your wealth, with the firstfruits of all your crops; then your barns will be filled to overflowing . . ."

" 'Do not store up for yourselves treasures on earth, where moth and rust destroy, and where thieves break in and steal. But store up for yourselves treasures in heaven, where moth and rust do not destroy, and where thieves do not break in and steal.' "

Matthew 6:19, 20

One of the greatest drawbacks to Christianity is the Christian's savings account. The rainy day is here. Give what you can, while you can, to share the Gospel of Christ. Forever, you will be glad.

"One man gives freely, yet gains even more; another withholds unduly, but comes to poverty."
Proverbs 11:24

Our gain is in giving out, not in holding back. "It is more blessed to give than to receive."

"In everything I did, I showed you that by this kind of hard work we must help the weak, remembering the words the Lord Jesus himself said: 'It is more blessed to give than to receive.' "
Acts 20:35

This may not fit in with our thinking, but it fits in with His planning. Do some giving and watch God.

"He who gives to the poor will lack nothing, but he who closes his eyes to them receives many curses."
Proverbs 28:27

People of means should look for opportunities to help the less fortunate, not hide from them. There is a feeling that comes with giving that has no comparison.

" 'There was a rich man who was dressed in purple and fine linen and lived in luxury every day.' "

Luke 16:19

Here was a man busy "living it up," not knowing that he would shortly be giving it up. Father, help us to turn our resources, including all that we are and all that we have, into something that is real and lasting. In Jesus' name. Amen.

"Then Jacob made a vow, saying, 'If God will be with me and will watch over me on this journey I am taking and will give me food to eat and clothes to wear . . . and this stone that I have set up as a pillar will be God's house, and of all that you give me I will give you a tenth.' "

Genesis 28:20, 22

There is something about getting right with God that associates itself with giving.

"There will always be poor people in the land. Therefore I command you to be open-handed toward your brothers and toward the poor and needy in your land."

Deuteronomy 15:11

The poor have a special place in the heart of God. Be good to them!

———————————

" 'I tell you the truth, whatever you did for one of the least of these brothers of mine, you did for me.' "

Matthew 25:40

Anyone wanting to do the Lord a personal favor can do so with an act of kindness to the least of His children. "Love is patient, love is kind."

———————————

" 'A tithe of everything from the land, whether grain from the soil or fruit from the trees, belongs to the Lord; it is holy to the Lord.' "

Leviticus 27:30

Every church ought to be supported by every member giving a minimum of the tithe of their income. "God loves a cheerful giver."

———————————

"Honor the Lord with your wealth, with the firstfruits of all your crops."

Proverbs 3:9

The work of God is plagued by big talkers and little givers. How can we expect God's best and give crumbs to the cause of Christ? "A tithe of everything . . . belongs to the Lord . . ."

"Therefore, I urge you, brothers, in view of God's mercy, to offer your bodies as living sacrifices, holy and pleasing to God — this is your spiritual act of worship."

Romans 12:1

We all need to be willing and living sacrifices content in offering ourselves to God. The Lord is not looking for people to die for Him, but to live for Him.

"Whoever tries to keep his life will lose it, and whoever loses his life will preserve it."

Luke 17:33

The only part of us that we can take with us is what we have given away.

"Blessed is he who has regard for the weak; the Lord delivers him in times of trouble. The Lord will protect him and preserve his life; he will bless him in the land and not surrender him to the desire of his foes."

Psalm 41:1, 2

The man who has a place in his heart for the unfortunate will be blessed of God and remembered by mankind. You can't out-give God. "Give, and it will be given to you."

———————————

"In everything I did, I showed you that by this kind of hard work we must help the weak, remembering the words the Lord Jesus himself said: 'It is more blessed to give than to receive.' "

Acts 20:35

Get in on the giving end. That's where God is. You will be the busiest man in town and the most blessed.

———————————

"And God is able to make all grace abound to you, so that in all things at all times, having all that you need, you will abound in every good work."

2 Corinthians 9:8

Be looking for places to give to the glory of God, and He will see to it that you have it to give. "God loves a cheerful giver."

———————

" 'Do not store up for yourselves treasures on earth, where moth and rust destroy, and where thieves break in and steal. But store up for yourselves treasures in heaven, where moth and rust do not destroy, and where thieves do not break in and steal. For where your treasure is, there your heart will be also.' "

Matthew 6:19-21

If you are looking for lasting dividends, you had better get something on deposit in Heaven. You can have what you want if you give enough.

———————

" 'Be careful not to do your 'acts of right-eousness' before men, to be seen by them. If you do, you will have no reward from your Father in heaven. . . . So that your giving may be in secret. Then your Father, who sees what is done in secret, will reward you.' "

Matthew 6:1, 4

There are many ways to give, but none is so graceful . . . and harder!

———————————

"He also saw a poor widow put in two very small copper coins. 'I tell you the truth,' he said, 'this poor widow has put in more than all the others. All these people gave their gifts out of their wealth; but she out of her poverty put in all she had to live on.' "

Luke 21:2-4

The Lord still sees the gift and the attitude of the giver. He also knows if you have reached a point of sacrifice in your giving. "God loves a cheerful giver." Attend your church and give to the cause of Christ through it, and pray for God's servant. He will bless you for it.

———————————

" 'Give, and it will be given to you. A good measure, pressed down, shaken together and running over, will be poured into your lap. For with the measure you use, it will be measured to you.' "

Luke 6:38

We can have what we want if we give enough! Our Father, give us great desire to give of ourselves and our means that we may know the reality of this good Word from You. In Jesus' name. Amen.

". . . I will give you a tenth."

Genesis 28:22

Man owes God at least ten percent of his income and all of his life.

"One man gives freely, yet gains even more; another withholds unduly, but comes to poverty. A generous man will prosper; he who refreshes others will himself be refreshed . . . He who seeks good finds goodwill, but evil comes to him who searches for it."

Proverbs 11:24, 25, 27

This is simply to say that giving does it, whether it is of ourselves or means. Be looking for ways and means to give, to our church first and then to as many worthy projects as possible.

"When I felt secure, I said, 'I will never be shaken.' "

Psalm 30:6

Look out! The One who gave it can take it away. Father, give us the spirit of generosity, knowing that we cannot outgive You. "Give, and it will be given to you."

"If a king judges the poor with fairness, his throne will always be secure."

Proverbs 29:14

Likewise, if we would find favor with God, we should look for some poor people to share His love and our means with.

God's Love....

God's Love

" 'For God so loved the world that he gave his one and only Son, that whoever believes in him shall not perish but have eternal life.' "

John 3:16

God's love is big enough to cover the world and yet individual enough so that the least of us are included.

———————————

"For I am convinced that neither death nor life, neither angels nor demons, neither the present nor the future, nor any powers, neither height nor depth, nor anything else in all creation, will be able to separate us from the love of God that is in Christ Jesus our Lord."

Romans 8:38, 39

He is not only a Saviour, but a keeper. "You will keep in perfect peace him whose mind is steadfast . . ."

———————————

"Hatred stirs up dissension, but love covers over all wrongs."

Proverbs 10:12

Love and hatred cannot abide together in the human heart. "By this all men will know

that you are my disciples, if you love one another." "Love covers a multitude of sins."

"Bestowing wealth on those who love me
and making their treasuries full."

Proverbs 8:21

Once our love and commitment to the
Lord is established, there is no end to what He
will do for us, and Jesus said, "through us."
"Seek first his kingdom and his righteousness,
and all these things will be given to you as
well."

" 'Righteous Father, though the world does
not know you, I know you, and they know that
you have sent me. I have made you known to
them, and will continue to make you known in
order that the love you have for me may be in
them and that I myself may be in them.' "

John 17:25, 26

Look how much we have going for us. We
were included in His prayer then. We are included now. ". . . he always lives to intercede
for them."

"Now the Lord God had planted a garden in the east, in Eden; and there he put the man he had formed."

Genesis 2:8

God, in His love, made man and put him in a garden. Man, in disobedience, hate, and sin, has created a jungle for himself. Only the Lord Jesus knows the way out! He provided it at the cross. "I am the way . . ."

───────────

"May those who delight in my vindication shout for joy and gladness; may they always say, 'The Lord be exalted, who delights in the well-being of his servant.' "

Psalm 35:27

Whoever heard of a king who wanted to work a hardship on one of his children? The Lord is the King of Kings, and everyone who has accepted His Son is entitled to what He has. He has made the provision, and He takes pleasure in seeing us prosper. Thank You, Lord, for it all.

───────────

Believe big! What you are asking is nothing compared to what He has already given. "Is any thing too hard for the Lord?"

———————————

" 'Though the mountains be shaken and the hills be removed, yet my unfailing love for you will not be shaken nor my covenant of peace be removed,' says the Lord, who has compassion on you."

Isaiah 54:10

Look at the words He uses to show that He loves you. Lose your fears and cares in the midst of this great promise.

———————————

"When they had crucified him, they divided up his clothes by casting lots. And sitting down, they kept watch over him there."

Matthew 27:35, 36

The death of Jesus was fulfilled prophecy, and foretold love. "God so loved . . . that he gave."

———————————

"Their hearts were not loyal to him, they were not faithful to his covenant. Yet he was merciful; he forgave their iniquities and did not destroy them. Time after time he restrained his anger and did not stir up his full wrath."

Psalm 78:37, 38

Isn't God good? In spite of our failings, He is ready to forgive. But remember, He said, "My Spirit will not contend with man forever . . ." "Today, if you hear his voice, do not harden your hearts . . ."

———————

" 'Praise be to the Lord, who has given rest to his people Israel just as he promised. Not one word has failed of all the good promises he gave through his servant Moses.' "

1 Kings 8:56

Look at the record and leave the rest to Him. He will keep His Word with you. We are but to claim it.

———————

"The Lord is gracious and compassionate, slow to anger and rich in love."

Psalm 145:8

He who said, "I have compassion for these people" is still interested in solving even the smallest problem. Earth has no sorrow that Heaven cannot heal.

———————————

" 'I, even I, am he who blots out your transgressions, for my own sake, and remembers your sins no more.' "

Isaiah 43:25

God is not like man, for after we have acknowledged our wrong, He remembers it no longer. To be forgiving is to be Godlike. To forget the past is to be even more like God.

———————————

"Cast all your anxiety on him because he cares for you."

1 Peter 5:7

The Lord will lift your burden if you will let go. Christ cares, but He cannot carry that which we refuse to commit to Him.

———————————

" '. . . No eye has seen, no ear has heard, no mind has conceived what God has prepared for those who love him.' "

1 Corinthians 2:9

Not only has He prepared the joys of this life for those who love Him, but at the end of our lives here, we will be amazed at what He has for us. Pass up that which seems to glitter in this life, but which in reality is out to rob us of God's best. Then in the end, you will see it was best for Him to have His way with thee.

———————————

" 'God, have mercy on me, a sinner.' "

Luke 18:13

Because He came to save that which was lost, He cannot do anything for us until we acknowledge our lost condition. Sin may be clasped so close, we cannot see its face.

———————————

"When I am afraid, I will trust in you."

Psalm 56:3

The love of God sets us free from the fear of man. "Thou art my shield and refuge."

———————————

" 'For God so loved the world that he gave his one and only Son, that whoever believes in him shall not perish but have eternal life.' "

John 3:16

The salvation of man cost God the death of His only Son. It is so unreasonable to think that man can ignore Him and incur the favor of the Father.

––––––––––––––

"I will say of the Lord, 'He is my refuge and my fortress, my God, in whom I trust.' "

Psalm 91:2

He is both a place to hide and abide. Come in out of the storm and strife of life regularly and meet with your Maker. You will be better equipped to face the world and do His work.

––––––––––––––

"All your fortresses are like fig trees with their first ripe fruit; when they are shaken, the figs fall into the mouth of the eater."

Nahum 3:12

In our rebellion toward God, it is well to remember what would happen if He withdrew His restraining hand of mercy and left us to our enemies.

———————

" 'If you, then, though you are evil, know how to give good gifts to your children, how much more will your Father in heaven give good gifts to those who ask him!' "

Matthew 7:11

We should not only be courageous in our asking, but confident of His answer.

———————

"I the Lord do not change. So you, O descendants of Jacob, are not destroyed."

Malachi 3:6

It is in our little thinking and lack of faith that the power and grace of God is past tense. Not so. He loves you, has a plan for your life and is the same yesterday, today, and forever.

———————

"For I am convinced that neither death nor life, neither angels nor demons, neither the present nor the future, nor any powers, neither height nor depth, nor anything else in all creation, will be able to separate us from the love of God that is in Christ Jesus our Lord."

Romans 8:38, 39

He is not only a Saviour, but a keeper. "You will keep in perfect peace him whose mind is steadfast . . ."

———————————

". . . may the Lord think of me."

Psalm 40:17

The great and eternal God has me in mind. How can I ignore Him? God said, "I have loved you with an everlasting love."

———————————

"How great is the love the Father has lavished on us, that we should be called children of God! And that is what we are! The reason the world does not know us is that it did not know him."

1 John 3:1

What a present, and what a future for the follower; and thank God, no past. Don't miss such a love!

———————————

"You have granted him the desire of his heart and have not withheld the request of his lips. *Selah*"
Psalm 21:2

The truth about God is that He is waiting and wanting to give. The trouble with us is that we think He has to be talked into it.

" 'For God so loved the world that he gave his one and only Son, that whoever believes in him shall not perish but have eternal life.' "
John 3:16

Here is the whole story of the old, old story. Take it to heart. It will take you to Heaven.

"I will give you the treasures of darkness, riches stored in secret places, so that you may know that I am the Lord, the God of Israel, who summons you by name."
Isaiah 45:3

"No good thing does he withhold from those whose walk is blameless." Father, guide Your children into all the prosperity that You planned for us spiritually and physically and give us a generous spirit to go with it. In Jesus' dear name. Amen.

"But God demonstrates his own love for us in this: While we were still sinners, Christ died for us."

Romans 5:8

Long before it was decided which way you were going, Jesus went to the cross to assure you of the abundant and eternal life. "He who has the Son has life; he who does not have the Son of God does not have life."

"The Lord your God is with you, he is mighty to save. He will take great delight in you, he will quiet you with his love, he will rejoice over you with singing."

Zephaniah 3:17

Don't be shaken by what you see and feel. Only consider the One standing by you. "I will never leave you or forsake you."

" 'Praise be to the Lord, who has given rest to his people Israel just as he promised. Not one word has failed of all the good promises he gave through his servant Moses.' "

1 Kings 8:56

God's Word is a great deal more than cold print. It is charged with the power of the Holy Ghost to bring into our lives might and miracles such as we have never known.

"Jesus replied, 'If anyone loves me, he will obey my teaching. My Father will love him, and we will come to him and make our home with him.' "

John 14:23

Behold the reward in the keeping of His Word! "We will come to him and make our home with him." What living . . . what love! ". . . The one who is in you is greater than the one who is in the world."

"The Lord your God is with you, he is mighty to save. He will take great delight in you, he will quiet you with his love, he will rejoice over you with singing."

Zephaniah 3:17

Don't ever think that you can stump God with big prayer requests. "Call to me and I will answer you and tell you great and unsearchable things you do not know." Praise God for His mighty acts.

"He who did not spare his own Son, but gave him up for us all — how will he not also, along with him, graciously give us all things?"

Romans 8:32

The love of God that gave us Jesus will not withhold anything else from us that would be for our good and His glory. "Dear friend, I pray that you may enjoy good health and that all may go well with you, even as your soul is getting along well."

"He will love you and bless you and increase your numbers. He will bless the fruit of your womb, the crops of your land — your grain, new wine and oil — the calves of your herds and the lambs of your flocks in the land that he swore to your forefathers to give you."

Deuteronomy 7:13

What a promise! What a fulfillment! "My word will not return unto me empty."

"Who forgives all your sins and heals all your diseases."

Psalm 103:3

All is covered, but we must come. "Come to me, all you who are weary and burdened, and I will give you rest." Father, touch the hurt and the needs of this reader in this moment. I ask in Jesus' mighty name. Amen.

――――――――――

" 'And even the very hairs of your head are all numbered.' "

Matthew 10:30

If you are inclined to think that you are unnoticed by the Lord, give this another reading. God loves you and has plans for your life. Ask Him what they are.

――――――――――

"May God himself, the God of peace, sanctify you through and through. May your whole spirit, soul and body be kept blameless at the coming of our Lord Jesus Christ. The one who calls you is faithful and he will do it."

1 Thessalonians 5:23, 24

God's grace is sufficient. Give it all over to Him . . . "who through faith are shielded by God's power until the coming of the salvation . . ."

"But he gives us more grace. That is why Scripture says: 'God opposes the proud but gives grace to the humble.' "

James 4:6

The humble stand moves the heart of God. "Humble yourselves before the Lord, and he will lift you up."

"But he said to me, 'My grace is sufficient for you, for my power is made perfect in weakness.' Therefore I will boast all the more gladly about my weaknesses, so that Christ's power may rest on me."

2 Corinthians 12:9

When we come to the end of ourselves, it is the beginning of Himself. "If God is for us, who can be against us?" Thanks, Lord, that it is not our strength but Yours that sees us through and over.

"He who did not spare his own Son, but gave him up for us all — how will he not also, along with him, graciously give us all things?"

Romans 8:32

This forever settles the issue that nothing is too much to ask of the Lord. If He went that far, and He did, to prove His love, He will go to any length to meet our needs. "I am the Lord, the God of all mankind. Is anything too hard for me?"

———————————

"Not that we are competent in ourselves to claim anything for ourselves, but our competence comes from God."

2 Corinthians 3:5

God is enough! He is the source of all that is good . . . and "No good thing does he withhold from those whose walk is blameless." "My grace is sufficient for you."

———————————

" 'I will be a Father to you, and you will be my sons and daughters, says the Lord Almighty.' "

2 Corinthians 6:18

When we consider the relationship we have with the Lord, it is all the more reason we should love and serve Him. "How great is the love the Father has lavished on us, that we should be called children of God! . . ."

———————

"I will cleanse them from all the sin they have committed against me and will forgive all their sins of rebellion against me."

Jeremiah 33:8

If you have ever wondered how far the love of God would go, take another look at this. "I have loved you with an everlasting love."

———————

"He who conceals his sins does not prosper, but whoever confesses and renounces them finds mercy."

Proverbs 28:13

The thing that may be holding us back is what we are hiding from God. Tell Him your problem. Whatever the problem, He is the answer. "If we confess our sins, he is faithful and just and will forgive us our sins and purify us from all unrighteousness."

———————

"Grace and peace be yours in abundance through the knowledge of God and of Jesus our Lord. His divine power has given us everything we need for life and godliness through our knowledge of him who called us by his own glory and goodness."

2 Peter 1:2, 3

God has touched every base of human need to give us a full and beautiful life all the way home. How strange that we find it so hard to believe and receive. Believe what He says. Take what He offers. Thanks, Lord.

———————————

Words of Guidance....

Words of Guidance

" 'Do to others as you would have them do to you.' "

Luke 6:31

Here is the beginning of the new world you have always wanted to create.

"A man's pride brings him low, but a man of lowly spirit gains honor."

Proverbs 29:23

Pride is a killer that has slain many spiritual giants. When a person gets wrapped up in himself, he makes a pretty small package.

"As you hold out the word of life — in order that I may boast on the day of Christ that I did not run or labor for nothing."

Philippians 2:16

Here's news, Christian friend. Our greatest job is not to explain the Word of God, but to extend it.

"May the words of my mouth and the meditation of my heart be pleasing in your sight, O Lord, my Rock and my Redeemer."

Psalm 19:14

Not only what we talk about, but what we think about, is screened by the Lord. Is it acceptable to the Lord?

"Do you see a man who speaks in haste? There is more hope for a fool than for him."

Proverbs 29:20

Hasty words lead to rash decisions resulting so often in heartbreak. Think a little before you say a lot. Man shall "give an account of every idle word."

"Do not set foot on the path of the wicked or walk in the way of evil men."

Proverbs 4:14

Don't ask for trouble by placing yourself in the path of the evildoer. We are in the world, but we don't have to be of it. Follow God's way as He says, "This is the way; walk in it."

". . . make them come in, so that my house will be full."

Luke 14:23

Put forth some effort for God. Recognize the urgency of the message that you have and find someone quick to tell it to. "Bring them in from the paths of sin." God's house is a hive for workers, not a rest for drones.

"You have lived on earth in luxury and self-indulgence. You have fattened yourselves in the day of slaughter."

James 5:5

Big times are not always good times. Only Jesus satisfies. "But seek first his kingdom and his righteousness, and all these things will be given to you as well."

"Commit your way to the Lord; trust in him and he will do this."

Psalm 37:5

The reason that the Lord doesn't bring a lot of things to pass is because He can't get past

us. Move over and let God take the lead. "How unsearchable his judgments, and his paths beyond tracing out!"

"So he gave them what they asked for, but sent a wasting disease upon them."

Psalm 106:15

This is a high price to pay for determination to have your own way. Let God rule. He knows best.

"Better a patient man than a warrior, a man who controls his temper than one who takes a city."

Proverbs 16:32

To be strong at these points is to please God, to promote harmony, and to have peace. What more could we ask?

"Keep your lives free from the love of money and be content with what you have, because God has said, 'Never will I leave you; never will I forsake you.'"

Hebrews 13:5

Use what you have while you live . . . for the glory of God and the good of mankind. This is the best way to keep it from having you.

"If my people, who are called by my name, will humble themselves and pray and seek my face and turn from their wicked ways, then will I hear from heaven and will forgive their sin and will heal their land."

2 Chronicles 7:14

God keeps coming back with the same prescription for recovery and we keep coming up with the same old postponement. "But seek first his kingdom and his righteousness, and all these things will be given to you as well."

"He went to Nazareth, where he had been brought up, and on the Sabbath day he went into the synagogue, as was his custom. And he stood up to read."

Luke 4:16

The next time you are inclined to think that the worship services at your church are not important, take another look at the Lord's practice. You need the church and the church needs you. "Let us not give up meeting together . . ."

"But the Lord said to me, 'Tell them, "Do not go up and fight, because I will not be with you. You will be defeated by your enemies." ' "

Deuteronomy 1:42

The person or nation that goes out to do battle with the forces of the world ought to be sure that they have the backing of Heaven. ". . . apart from me you can do nothing."

". . . Lot lived among the cities of the plain and pitched his tents near Sodom."

Genesis 13:12

People who pitch their tent in the direction of evil ought not be surprised at the outcome after they have arrived.

" 'But seek first his kingdom and his right-eousness, and all these things will be given to you as well.' "

Matthew 6:33

Our great problem has ever been to put material things in their right place. Let nothing keep you from your church and away from Christ.

" 'No one can serve two masters. Either he will hate the one and love the other, or he will be devoted to the one and despise the other. You cannot serve both God and Money.' "

Matthew 6:24

Man must make a clean break from the world if he is to have a close tie with Heaven.

"So then, just as you received Christ Jesus as Lord, continue to live in him."

Colossians 2:6

It is as important to keep Him in our walk as it is to keep Him in our worship. A sermon in shoes stands out.

"Bless those who persecute you; bless and do not curse."

Romans 12:14

There is no cure like kindness. Shock your enemy; return a little good for evil and you will be in for a surprise yourself.

———————————

"Anyone who welcomes him shares in his wicked work."

2 John 11

Many of us pat evil on the back by not saying a word. Silence can also be sinful.

———————————

"There is a way that seems right to a man, but in the end it leads to death."

Proverbs 14:12

The unconverted man who follows his own conscience without conviction is on shaky ground. Let God guide you.

———————————

"Commit your way to the Lord; trust in him and he will do this."

Psalm 37:5

Our real strength lies in our wholehearted surrender to His will and way. "Be strong in the Lord . . ."

———————————

" 'Again, the kingdom of heaven is like a merchant looking for fine pearls. When he found one of great value, he went away and sold everything he had and bought it.' "

Matthew 13:45, 46

This is a lesson in majoring in main things. Put all that you have and all that you are in the one and only thing that really counts.

———————————

"Do not make any gods to be alongside me; do not make for yourselves gods of silver or gods of gold."

Exodus 20:23

Gold makes a poor god and an overbearing master. "But seek first his kingdom and his righteousness, and all these things will be given to you as well."

———————————

" '. . . do to others what you would have them do to you . . .' "

Matthew 7:12

Here are eleven words that can change our lives.

". . . that you may live a life worthy of the Lord and may please him in every way: bearing fruit in every good work, growing in the knowledge of God."

Colossians 1:10

We would really be doing something if our study and dedication to God's Word would keep step with our great search for education.

"If my people, who are called by my name, will humble themselves and pray and seek my face and turn from their wicked ways, then will I hear from heaven and will forgive their sin and will heal their land."

2 Chronicles 7:14

Mr. Candidate, bring this great truth home to us as Americans, and God will honor you. Here is the platform that will never crumble. Take your stand here and take it to the American people. "Righteousness exalts a nation, but sin is a disgrace to any people."

"The fear of the Lord is the beginning of knowledge, but fools despise wisdom and discipline."

Proverbs 1:7

This says something to the so-called intellectual who has completely ignored the main stream of real science and common sense and has branched off in pursuit of knowledge without God.

"Jotham grew powerful because he walked steadfastly before the Lord his God."

2 Chronicles 27:6

Power belongeth to God and is available to man. The man who does not take God into account in his preparation for life will have to reckon with Him as to why he didn't.

―――――――――

" 'Do not judge, and you will not be judged. Do not condemn, and you will not be condemned. Forgive, and you will be forgiven.' "

Luke 6:37

Before we can be cleansed of our own faults, we must have everything in the clear with our neighbor. "But if you do not forgive men their sins, your Father will not forgive your sins."

―――――――――

"Wisdom is supreme; therefore get wisdom. Though it cost all you have, get understanding."

Proverbs 4:7

We live in a world that has gone wild about everything but wisdom. Father God, give us wisdom, will power, and a desire that we have not as yet known to please You and win the world to Jesus. In His name and for Your glory. Amen.

―――――――――

"Blessed is the man who does not walk in the counsel of the wicked or stand in the way of sinners or sit in the seat of mockers."

Psalm 1:1

Find a man who is well disciplined at these three points and you will find a real disciple of God, though he may not say a word.

"A man finds joy in giving an apt reply — and how good is a timely word!"

Proverbs 15:23

The right word at the right time can really turn a situation around. Pray that it will come to you.

"Better a patient man than a warrior, a man who controls his temper than one who takes a city."

Proverbs 16:32

The "in fighting" is what's rough. Win there and the victory is yours. Call up the inner man. ". . . the one who is in you is greater than the one who is in the world."

"The sluggard craves and gets nothing, but the desires of the diligent are fully satisfied."

Proverbs 13:4

There is a lot to be said for doing, as well as dreaming. ". . . faith by itself, if it is not accompanied by action, is dead." Work while it is day. The night cometh when no man can work.

"When a man's ways are pleasing to the Lord, he makes even his enemies live at peace with him."

Proverbs 16:7

Here is another good reason for putting the Lord first. "But seek first his kingdom and his righteousness, and all these things will be given to you as well."

"Good understanding wins favor, but the way of the unfaithful is hard."

Proverbs 13:15

If for some reason you have gotten the idea that living the good life is hard, take another look at this truth. You will never relive today. Make it a good one with God's help!

"If only you would be altogether silent! For you, that would be wisdom."

Job 13:5

Many times, saying nothing is about the smartest thing we can do.

"See to it that no one misses the grace of God and that no bitter root grows up to cause trouble and defile many."

Hebrews 12:15

We must fight negative thought patterns and poutings or else they will neutralize our lives, leaving us ineffective and miserable. Cheer up! God loves you and has plans for you beyond your greatest dreams.

"After that, we who are still alive and are left will be caught up together with them in the clouds to meet the Lord in the air. And so we will be with the Lord forever."

1 Thessalonians 4:17

Every Christian ought to be ready to go on a moment's notice and yet willing to work a lifetime waiting for His return. "Even so, come, Lord Jesus!"

"Don't let anyone look down on you because you are young, but set an example for the believers in speech, in life, in love, in faith and in purity."

1 Timothy 4:12

Life is a book of memories we start writing early to be read over and over again. Happy is the person who enjoys what he has written even when he is old.

―――――――――

"Do not fret because of evil men or be envious of those who do wrong."

Psalm 37:1

It is easy to get so wrapped up in condemning evil that we grow negligent in doing good.

―――――――――

". . . when he comes in his glory and in the glory of the Father and of the holy angels."

Luke 9:26

Don't think that you can ignore the Lord in this life and have Him make a lot over you in the life to come.

―――――――――

". . . 'Let us go with you, because we have heard that God is with you.' "

Zechariah 8:23

When you find a man who shows evidence of walking with the Lord, you will do well to join him. Make friends with those who are friends of God.

———————

"Each one should remain in the situation which he was in when God called him."

1 Corinthians 7:20

Every person has a place in life to fill and he has no peace until he finds it. Let God's will be your way.

———————

". . . you ignored all my advice and would not accept my rebuke."

Proverbs 1:25

The person traveling with a one-track mind is bound to have a head-on collision.

———————

"Teach us to number our days aright, that we may gain a heart of wisdom."

Psalm 90:12

Life is serious and should be lived seriously. That doesn't mean that all the pleasure is taken out of it. But it has a lot to do with cutting the mistakes to a minimum.

"Don't grumble against each other, brothers, or you will be judged. The Judge is standing at the door!"

James 5:9

Give up the grudge. It is not worth it. Too many victories have gone by the way already. "But if you do not forgive men their sins, your Father will not forgive your sins."

"The one who sows to please his sinful nature, from that nature will reap destruction; the one who sows to please the Spirit, from the Spirit will reap eternal life."

Galatians 6:8

Life is a matter of sowing and reaping, and it is given to every man to determine the crop.

"No, in all these things we are more than conquerors through him who loved us."

Romans 8:37

Let us act like what God says we are, and watch despair disappear.

"Let us not give up meeting together, as some are in the habit of doing, but let us encourage one another — and all the more as you see the Day approaching."

Hebrews 10:25

If we could only see the value of obedience to God in this area, there would be such a run on the church that it would alarm the world and amaze the believer. Attend the Lord's house this week with your family. The rest of the week will go better at your house.

"Be kind and compassionate to one another, forgiving each other, just as in Christ God forgave you."

Ephesians 4:32

The life and example of Christ is not only to be admired, but followed.

"I urge, then, first of all, that requests, prayers, intercession and thanksgiving be made for everyone — for kings and all those in authority, that we may live peaceful and quiet lives in all godliness and holiness."

1 Timothy 2:1, 2

This is not a suggestion, but a directive. Let us obey. Father, we go beyond party lines as we put all elected officials on the prayer line. In this moment, we pray for our President and every other official, their families and the people they represent. Bless them with health, wisdom and spiritual perception through Jesus Christ our Lord. Amen.

———————

" 'Therefore I tell you, do not worry about your life, what you will eat or drink; or about your body, what you will wear. Is not life more important than food, and the body more important than clothes?' "

Matthew 6:25

Here is where we put the most emphasis and Jesus said where we should put the least. "But seek first his kingdom and his righteousness, and all these things will be given to you as well."

———————

" 'Do to others as you would have them do to you.' "

Luke 6:31

Behold the great prescription of life! When properly administered and taken, it can clear up every disease of ill will known to man. We get the real picture of life as we major in the art of putting ourselves in each other's place.

———————

"Then do this, my son, to free yourself, since you have fallen into your neighbor's hands: Go and humble yourself; press your plea with your neighbor!"

Proverbs 6:3

Take the humble position. The hardest things to do are very often the most rewarding.

———————

The Holy Spirit....

The Holy Spirit

" 'When the Counselor comes, whom I will send to you from the Father, the Spirit of truth who goes out from the Father, he will testify about me.' "

John 15:26

The Holy Spirit is our constant companion and our Divine Teacher whose number one assignment is pointing us to Jesus. When we have learned that lesson, we will have pleased the Teacher, received power in our lives, and fulfilled the plan of the Father.

———————

"But you will receive power when the Holy Spirit comes on you; and you will be my witnesses in Jerusalem, and in all Judea and Samaria, and to the ends of the earth."

Acts 1:8

Too long have we tried to produce on our own power and have discovered that we have the wrong connection and the lines were down. We must be filled with the Spirit or be content with human frustration.

"So he sent and had him brought in. He was ruddy, with a fine appearance and handsome features.

Then the Lord said, 'Rise and anoint him; he is the one.'

So Samuel took the horn of oil and anointed him in the presence of his brothers, and from that day on the Spirit of the Lord came upon David in power. . . ."

1 Samuel 16:12, 13

The Spirit of the Lord upon a man is still the best credential that he can have . . . and probably the only one that God recognizes.

———————

"The Lord will guide you always; he will satisfy your needs in a sun-scorched land and will strengthen your frame. You will be like a well-watered garden, like a spring whose waters never fail."

Isaiah 58:11

God guides us through the inspiration of His Word, the inner impression of His presence and through circumstances that He has created or allowed. The Holy Spirit will guide you into all truth. Let Him!

" 'If you then, though you are evil, know how to give good gifts to your children, how much more will your Father in heaven give the Holy Spirit to those who ask him!' "

Luke 11:13

With the thought in mind that God is surely as concerned and capable as you are in also giving you His best, simply open your heart and receive. ". . . no good thing does he withhold from those whose walk is blameless."

"I would not have known him, except that the one who sent me to baptize with water told me, 'The man on whom you see the Spirit come down and remain is he who will baptize with the Holy Spirit.' "

John 1:33

There is no spiritual experience outside of the Saviour.

"As he spoke, the Spirit came into me and raised me to my feet, and I heard him speaking to me."

Ezekiel 2:2

When the Spirit of God enters the human life, it becomes the vessel through which God speaks and lives are touched.

———————

" 'But you will receive power when the Holy Spirit comes on you; and you will be my witnesses in Jerusalem, and in all Judea and Samaria, and to the ends of the earth.' "

Acts 1:8

It's God's Holy Spirit that gives us something to say and the power to go with it. How futile to keep struggling in the flesh. Holy Spirit, fill us with Your presence and send us out with Your power in the service of God, in Jesus' name. Amen.

———————

"In the same way, the Spirit helps us in our weakness. We do not know what we ought to pray for, but the Spirit himself intercedes for us with groans that words cannot express. And he who searches our hearts knows the mind of the Spirit, because the Spirit intercedes for the saints in accordance with God's will."

Romans 8:26, 27

Invite the Holy Spirit to intercede for you and through you. You will discover it is a passing gear and an overdrive in your prayer life far beyond what you ever dreamed possible.

———————

"So he said to me, 'This is the word of the Lord to Zerubbabel: "Not by might nor by power, but by my Spirit," says the Lord Almighty.' "

Zechariah 4:6

Simply turn it over to the Holy Spirit. He takes the strain and suspense out of it all. Oh Holy Spirit, in Jesus' name and for the glory of God, move in and through us and do what Jesus would be doing if He were here in person. In His name, Amen.

———————

"And afterward, I will pour out my Spirit on all people. Your sons and daughters will prophesy, your old men will dream dreams, your young men will see visions. Even on my servants, both men and women, I will pour out my Spirit in those days."

Joel 2:28, 29

We can see the evidence of that day in our time and, though many cannot understand it, none of us can deny it. Holy Spirit, breathe on us and empower us to evangelize the world in our time. In Jesus' name, Amen.

———————

" '. . . Not by might nor by power, but by my Spirit,' says the Lord Almighty."

Zechariah 4:6

We are guilty of depending on our own working and wisdom, and not depending upon the Holy Spirit and His power. If we would be happy in our Christian experience, we need to relieve ourselves of the strain of so many works of our own and submit all to the guidance of the Holy Spirit.

———————

"And the Spirit of the Lord began to stir him . . ."

Judges 13:25

Don't be satisfied with an occasional moving of the Spirit when we can have showers of blessing all the time. The anointing of the Spirit requires an ignoring of self.

———————————

"So he said to me, 'This is the word of the Lord to Zerubbabel: "Not by might nor by power, but by my Spirit," says the Lord Almighty.' "

Zechariah 4:6

No program, project or person can ever take the place of the Holy Spirit. The sooner the Church replaces the strain of pushing with the Spirit's leading, the easier our task will be.

———————————

" 'I am going to send you what my Father has promised; but stay in the city until you have been clothed with power from on high.' "

Luke 24:49

The Lord never meant for us to work for Him under our own power. Our lack of success

can probably be traced to the fact that we leaned on self and ignored the Spirit.

―――――――――

"Do not put out the Spirit's fire."
1 Thessalonians 5:19

There is no substitute for the Spirit of God. "And if anyone does not have the Spirit of Christ, he does not belong to Christ."

―――――――――

" 'For the Holy Spirit will teach you at that time what you should say.' "
Luke 12:12

Rely on the Holy Spirit. He has both the answer and the authority of the Father. ". . . the one who is in you is greater than the one who is in the world."

―――――――――

"The Lord replied, 'My Presence will go with you, and I will give you rest.' "
Exodus 33:14

The Lord's power, pardon and presence is available.

―――――――――

" 'You stiff-necked people, with uncircumcised hearts and ears! You are just like your fathers: You always resist the Holy Spirit!' "

Acts 7:51

This is part of a sermon that needs repeating often. It is a dangerous thing to resist the Holy Spirit. "My Spirit will not contend with man forever . . ." "Today, if you hear his voice, do not harden your hearts . . ."

"But the fruit of the Spirit is love, joy, peace, patience, kindness, goodness, faithfulness, gentleness and self-control. Against such things there is no law."

Galatians 5:22, 23

Here are the fruits of the Spirit, the outgrowth of the indwelling of His great presence. "By this all men will know that you are my disciples, if you love one another."

"We have not received the spirit of the world but the Spirit who is from God, that we may understand what God has freely given us."

1 Corinthians 2:12

Thank God for all the promises we have in Him. Jesus made them all possible. The Spirit of God makes them all known.

––––––––––––

"To one there is given through the Spirit the message of wisdom, to another the message of knowledge by means of the same Spirit . . . to another miraculous powers, to another prophecy, to another distinguishing between spirits, to another speaking in different kinds of tongues, and to still another the interpretation of tongues."
1 Corinthians 12:8, 10

Here are the gifts of the Spirit, given to be shared as starters for all else that God has for those who open up themselves to be used of Him.

––––––––––––

"In the same way, the Spirit helps us in our weakness. We do not know what we ought to pray for, but the Spirit himself intercedes for us with groans that words cannot express."

Romans 8:26

When we pray in the Spirit, we get to the heart of the matter! Holy Spirit, take our thoughts and our tongues and pray through us that we may touch God with our real need in Jesus' name, Amen.

―――――――――

"As for you, the anointing you received from him remains in you, and you do not need anyone to teach you. But as his anointing teaches you about all things and as that anointing is real, not counterfeit — just as it has taught you, remain in him."

1 John 2:27

Stop looking at what is going on around you and draw upon the strength of His Spirit who lives within you. ". . . the one who is in you is greater than the one who is in the world."

―――――――――

"And if the Spirit of him who raised Jesus from the dead is living in you, he who raised Christ from the dead will also give life to your mortal bodies through his Spirit, who lives in you."

Romans 8:11

Look at the power of the Holy Spirit! And if you are a Christian, He is in you to bring to pass all the powerful things that God meant for you to have.

———————

Jesus, Lord and Saviour....

Jesus, Lord and Saviour

". . . 'This is my Son, whom I love; with him I am well pleased.' "

Matthew 3:17

Jesus came into the world, lived under great hardships and died on the cross to satisfy His Father. What have you done to please Him?

_____

" 'But a Samaritan, as he traveled, came where the man was; and when he saw him, he took pity on him. He went to him and bandaged his wounds, pouring on oil and wine. Then he put the man on his own donkey, took him to an inn and took care of him.' "

Luke 10:33, 34

This is like Jesus. He always comes to where we are with all that we need and just in time. Don't worry about the ones who have passed you by. Think about the One who has gone all the way for you.

_____

"Jesus answered, 'I am the way and the truth and the life. No one comes to the Father except through me.' "

John 14:6

Jesus is the way to eternal life and any detour that we make for ourselves will only lead to a dead end. Ask Him boldly how to bless you with His presence and He will. "Here I am! I stand at the door and knock. If anyone hears my voice and opens the door, I will come in . . ."

" 'No one ever spoke the way this man does' . . ."

John 7:46

No one ever talked like Jesus; no one ever walked like Jesus; no one ever cared like Jesus.

"God has raised this Jesus to life, and we are all witnesses of the fact."

Acts 2:32

Death, man's most dreaded enemy, has become a servant instead of a slave master, all because of the love of God and the sacrifice of His Son. "Where, O death, is your sting?" "Because I live, you also will live."

". . . 'Who is this? Even the wind and the waves obey him!' "

Mark 4:41

Man can report the weather, but only God can do anything about it. Turn your storm-tossed life over to the One who will banish every fear. "So do not fear, for I am with you."

———————

"The men who were guarding Jesus began mocking and beating him."

Luke 22:63

Today, Jesus is mocked and crucified anew by unbelief and indifference by a self-sufficient world and a lukewarm Church.

———————

"Jesus said to her, 'I am the resurrection and the life. He who believes in me will live, even though he dies.' "

John 11:25

Jesus conquered death and claims the same victory for all who confess Him as Saviour. "Where, O death, is your sting? Where, O grave, is your victory?"

———————

"But God demonstrates his own love for us in this: While we were still sinners, Christ died for us."

Romans 5:8

The Lord takes us as we are to make us what we ought to be and what we really want to be. Christ is not only the answer, but the difference.

———————

"Jesus Christ is the same yesterday and today and forever."

Hebrews 13:8

Once a person really believes that Christ is the same, he himself will never be the same.

———————

"If we endure, we will also reign with him. If we disown him, he will also disown us."

2 Timothy 2:12

Don't put the Lord in the background here and expect Him to make a fuss over you in Heaven. The Saviour that you deny here will be the Saviour that you will meet in eternity.

———————

"May I never boast except in the cross of our Lord Jesus Christ . . ."

Galatians 6:14

The Lord takes us as we are to make us what we ought to be and what we really want to be. Christ is not only the answer, but the difference.

". . . And he will be called Wonderful Counselor, Mighty God, Everlasting Father, Prince of Peace."

Isaiah 9:6

He has been true to His name and true to His Word. He is qualified to help you in every area of life. Trust Him today!

"He himself bore our sins in his body on the tree . . ."

1 Peter 2:24

The sins of the whole world were borne by the Saviour, but every person must come individually to the cross to secure the pardon. He will set you free.

" 'I am the bread of life.' "

John 6:48

Only the Saviour can fully satisfy the longing soul and the burdened heart. He still feeds the hungry multitudes in life's wilderness.

" 'I am the Living One; I was dead, and behold I am alive for ever and ever! And I hold the keys of death and Hades.' "

Revelation 1:18

The living Christ is at the right hand of the living God, ready to save a world dead in trespasses and sins.

" 'The thief comes only to steal and kill and destroy; I have come that they may have life, and have it to the full.' "

John 10:10

God is for us having the good things of life. This is why Jesus came. Why settle for less?

"And from Jesus Christ, who is the faithful witness, the firstborn from the dead, and the ruler of the kings of the earth. To him who loves us and has freed us from our sins by his blood, and has made us to be a kingdom and priests to serve his God and Father — to him be glory and power for ever and ever! Amen."

Revelation 1:5, 6

There was only one way to deal with the sin problem, and Jesus became the answer. Turn it all over to Him. The cleansing is complete and it is free. He is faithful and just to cleanse us from all sin.

"But God demonstrates his own love for us in this: While we were still sinners, Christ died for us. Since we have now been justified by his blood, how much more shall we be saved from God's wrath through him!"

Romans 5:8, 9

The death of Jesus could not wait on our decision. He died in advance of what we would do. Even at this late date, "What will you do with Jesus?"

"On the last and greatest day of the Feast, Jesus stood and said in a loud voice, 'If anyone is thirsty, let him come to me and drink.' "

John 7:37

Here is the real thirst slaker. If you are weary of the desert and tired of the search, turn to the divine Saviour who will meet your need and forgive your sins.

"Night and day among the tombs and in the hills he would cry out and cut himself with stones.
When he saw Jesus from a distance, he ran and fell on his knees in front of him."

Mark 5:5, 6

Here is the story of a man who got tired of living in the scary surroundings of the tombs and came to the Saviour for relief. Are you living on an island in the tombs of fear and doubt? There is more to life than that. Jesus is coming your way. Receive Him.

"Now while he was in Jerusalem at the Passover Feast, many people saw the miraculous signs he was doing and believed in his name."

John 2:23

He was a miracle worker then. He is a miracle worker forever. "Jesus Christ is the same yesterday and today and forever."

———————

" 'Whoever believes in him is not condemned, but whoever does not believe stands condemned already because he has not believed in the name of God's one and only Son.' "

John 3:18

The unbeliever's future is already settled. Only an act of faith in the acceptance of Jesus Christ can regenerate him and reverse his destiny.

———————

"Jesus replied, 'You do not realize now what I am doing, but later you will understand.' "

John 13:7

It's not all that important that we know all that He does, so long as we are sure we know Him.

———————

"Yet to all who received him, to those who believed in his name, he gave the right to become children of God."

John 1:12

Our right relation with God is contingent upon what we do with His Son.

"And a voice from heaven said, 'This is my Son, whom I love; with him I am well pleased.'"

Matthew 3:17

It seems so incredible that so much of earth should ignore what all of Heaven has endorsed. "For God so loved the world that he gave his one and only Son . . ."

"Yet to all who received him, to those who believed in his name, he gave the right to become children of God."

John 1:12

A strained relationship between you and the Saviour is a sure separator between you and God. Jesus said, "No one comes to the Father except through me."

"He himself bore our sins in his body on the tree, so that we might die to sins and live for righteousness; by his wounds you have been healed."

1 Peter 2:24

The death of Jesus Christ upon the cross carried with it an atonement for soul and body. The sad report of so many of us is that we are reluctant to trust Him for either.

" 'She will give birth to a son, and you are to give him the name Jesus, because he will save his people from their sins.' "

Matthew 1:21

The whole world can sympathize, but only Jesus can save. Jesus saves, keeps and satisfies.

" 'The thief comes only to steal and kill and destroy; I have come that they may have life, and have it to the full.' "

John 10:10

Life really begins at the age when the "Rock of Ages" takes over. Contrary to what you may think, the Lord is in favor of you

having more of life, not less, and more reason to live it. You can live it up all the way to Heaven.

"And being found in appearance as a man, he humbled himself and became obedient to death — even death on a cross!"

Philippians 2:8

We must never forget that it took Christ going to the cross to cancel out our sins. It is not until we come to Him that we become a part of what He has provided.

"In whom we have redemption, the forgiveness of sins."

Colossians 1:14

In Jesus we have redemption, release, reward, and the revelation of the Father. It's all in Him and, without Him, all is in vain.

"Yet to all who received him, to those who believed in his name, he gave the right to become children of God."

John 1:12

We become a part of the family of God based on our relations with His Son.

———————

"But thanks be to God! He gives us the victory through our Lord Jesus Christ."

1 Corinthians 15:57

Too much time is spent on planning battles and fighting wars that have already been won. Take what He gives and give what He asks.

———————

"And when Jesus had cried out again in a loud voice, he gave up his spirit."

Matthew 27:50

We must never forget that Calvary was full of pain as well as pardon. "Christ suffered for us."

———————

" 'I am the bread of life. Your forefathers ate the manna in the desert, yet they died. But here is the bread that comes down from heaven, which a man may eat and not die.' "

John 6:48-50

There is no hunger like soul hunger, and there is nothing that will satisfy it but the Saviour. "Come and have breakfast . . ."

———————

"But this is to fulfill what is written in their Law: 'They hated me without reason.' "

John 15:25

Don't be so hard on people who rejected the Saviour in the past. If up to this point you have not accepted Him, you are in the same company. Why have you rejected Him? Right now, ask Him to come into your heart and He will.

———————

"For no one can lay any foundation other than the one already laid, which is Jesus Christ."

1 Corinthians 3:11

Nothing can be added to what our Divine Advocate did. To mix anything man-made as a means of our Salvation is to insult God and sink all hopes of our eternal life with Him.

———————

"When he was accused by the chief priests and the elders, he gave no answer."

Matthew 27:12

The answer of Jesus was in His submission to the crucifixion for the sins of all. By His death and resurrection, He is still speaking to all who are bound in sin and seeking to go free.

———————

"They spit on him, and took the staff and struck him on the head again and again.

After they had mocked him, they took off the robe and put his own clothes on him. Then they led him away to crucify him."

Matthew 27:30, 31

While it may seem unbelievable that it could happen, it is equally unbelievable that so many could forget it! "Christ died for our sins . . ."

"Jesus said to her, 'I am the resurrection and the life. He who believes in me will live, even though he dies.' "

John 11:25

Keep remembering that He is the giver of life and the master of death. "Because I live, you also will live."

"Day after day, in the temple courts and from house to house, they never stopped teaching and proclaiming the good news that Jesus is the Christ."

Acts 5:42

He was all of it! If we are to experience what they enjoyed, the emphasis must again be placed upon Jesus. "Salvation is found in no one else, for there is no other name under heaven given to man by which we must be saved."

"He replied, 'You of little faith, why are you so afraid?' Then he got up and rebuked the winds and the waves, and it was completely calm."

Matthew 8:26

No man can afford to face the storms of life without the Divine Captain. His presence alone brings calmness, confidence, and courage.

———————————

" 'If you believed Moses, you would believe me, for he wrote about me.' "

John 5:46

The whole world of God revolves around His Son, our Saviour. Our whole destiny depends on what we believe about it and what we do about it. "If you do not believe that I am the one I claim to be, you will indeed die in your sins."

———————————

"Jesus answered, 'I am the way and the truth and the life. No one comes to the Father except through me.' "

John 14:6

Jesus is not a way among many ways, but THE way. How foolish to look for detours.

———————————

" 'Woman,' he said, 'why are you crying? Who is it you are looking for?' "

John 20:15

The only One who can heal the broken heart is interested in every tear and every trial. ". . . he cares for you."

"He makes me lie down in green pastures, he leads me beside quiet waters."

Psalm 23:2

Only the Saviour can take the strain out of life . . . and the fear out of death.

"To him who is able to keep you from falling and to present you before his glorious presence without fault and with great joy."

Jude 24

He is not only a Saviour, but a keeper. "Praise the Lord."

"Yet to all who received him, to those who believed in his name, he gave the right to become children of God."

John 1:12

Our right relation with God is contingent upon what we do with His Son.

———————

"Jesus answered, 'I am the way and the truth and the life. No one comes to the Father except through me.' "

John 14:6

No man ignores the Son and reaches the Father. ". . . whoever rejects the Son will not see life, for God's wrath remains on him."

———————

" 'Come, see a man who told me everything I ever did. Could this be the Christ?' "

John 4:29

It is a sobering thing to know that the One you may be rejecting knows you so well and holds the power of life and death over you.

———————

"And she gave birth to her firstborn, a son. She wrapped him in cloths and placed him in a manger, because there was no room for them in the inn."

Luke 2:7

Our lives are like inns along the road of life, and Jesus is still at the door, waiting to come in and occupy His rightful place. Make room for Him.

———————

"Thomas said to him, 'Lord, we don't know where you are going, so how can we know the way?' "

John 14:5

Jesus saith unto him, "I am the way and the truth and the life. No one comes to the Father except through me."

———————

"And Mary said: 'My soul glorifies the Lord.' "

Luke 1:46

How wonderful it would be if we stopped magnifying the church, creeds and the credentials of man, and simply magnified Jesus Christ.

———————

"Therefore, since we have a great high priest who has gone through the heavens, Jesus the Son of God, let us hold firmly to the faith we profess."

Hebrews 4:14

There is nothing on the earth that our Saviour in Heaven can't handle. He ever liveth to make intercession for us.

"After his suffering, he showed himself to these men and gave many convincing proofs that he was alive. He appeared to them over a period of forty days and spoke about the kingdom of God."

Acts 1:3

It is a matter of record that He lived, died, and rose again. He now lives at the right hand of the Father and in the hearts of believers. ". . . he has risen, just as he said."

"For to us a child is born, to us a son is given, and the government will be on his shoulders. And he will be called Wonderful Counselor, Mighty God, Everlasting Father, Prince of Peace."

Isaiah 9:6

The world would breathe easier if God had more of a part in the governments today,

and as for that matter, if He had more of a prominent part in our churches.

―――――――

"See to it that no one takes you captive through hollow and deceptive philosophy, which depends on human tradition and the basic principles of this world rather than on Christ."

Colossians 2:8

If what you know or hear in the name of Christianity does not exalt Christ and glorify God, put it down as man made and not Heaven sent. The Holy Spirit is our ally of discernment and will direct us.

―――――――

"Who is he that condemns? Christ Jesus, who died — more than that, who was raised to life — is at the right hand of God and is also interceding for us."

Romans 8:34

We need to keep remembering that it was Jesus who died for our sins, and that He is alive, forevermore interceding for us.

―――――――

"And whatever you do, whether in word or deed, do it all in the name of the Lord Jesus, giving thanks to God the Father through him."

Colossians 3:17

If we want to make what we do count, it must be done in Christ's name and for His cause and with thanks.

———————

"In whom we have redemption, the forgiveness of sins."

Colossians 1:14

Nothing less and nothing more can settle the sin question in our lives. The blood of Jesus Christ, God's Son, cleanseth us from all sins. The application is in acknowledging that He died for us and we cannot really live without Him.

———————

Love....

Love

"So I will very gladly spend for you everything I have and expend myself as well. If I love you more, will you love me less?"

2 Corinthians 12:15

This is the only language that a confused world understands. A love that is not only vocal, but active. It is not what we say, but what we do that counts.

———————————

"Therefore, he who rejects this instruction does not reject man but God, who gives you his Holy Spirit."

1 Thessalonians 4:8

Our attitude toward our earthly brother is a good indication how we actually feel toward our Heavenly Father. "Love one another."

———————————

". . . to love your neighbor as yourself is more important than all burnt offerings and sacrifices."

Mark 12:33

It's not what we offer up, but what we think of our fellow man that impresses God. Money without mercy is meaningless.

———————————

"And he has given us this command: Whoever loves God must also love his brother."
1 John 4:21

God accepts no love that includes Him and excludes our fellow man. This is the identifying mark of a Christian. Does the world recognize you as such?

———————

"For Christ's love compels us . . ."
2 Corinthians 5:14

Self gives way to the Saviour when the love of Christ gets control of the heart. What the world needs today is more compassion and less censure.

———————

"Love is patient, love is kind. It does not envy, it does not boast, it is not proud."
1 Corinthians 13:4

Here is a test of true love. It's not all of it, but enough to let us know if we have the real thing.

———————

"But Ruth replied, 'Don't urge me to leave you or to turn back from you. Where you go I will go, and where you stay I will stay. Your people will be my people and your God my God.' "

Ruth 1:16

Love is a mysterious force imparted by God the Father and gloriously shared by His creatures to degrees beyond human comprehension and reason. No wonder the Lord said of the first Christians, "By this all men will know that you are my disciples, if you love one another."

" 'But I tell you: Love your enemies and pray for those who persecute you.' "

Matthew 5:44

If the spirit of Christ surfaces at this point in your life, you will know that you have done more than joined a church. All men will know that "You are my disciples, if you love one another."

" 'Teacher, which is the greatest commandment in the Law?' Jesus replied: 'Love the Lord your God with all your heart and with all your soul and with all your mind. This is the first and greatest commandment. And the second is like it: Love your neighbor as yourself.' "

Matthew 22:36-39

The reason the world is in trouble today is because we have made so little over the great commandment. "Love covers over a multitude of sins."

"Now about brotherly love we do not need to write to you, yourselves have been taught by God to love each other."
1 Thessalonians 4:9

It is not religious talk, but the love of God relived in Christian acts of the believer that will win this world to Jesus. "In word and deed . . ."

"When they saw the courage of Peter and John and realized that they were unschooled, ordinary men, they were astonished and they took note that these men had been with Jesus."
Acts 4:13

Do something Christ-like! Love people. It is not only have we told someone about Jesus, but have we shown them.

"A friend loves at all times, and a brother is born for adversity."

Proverbs 17:17

There ought to be a day set aside as "good friend day," and they should be told so. Today would be a good day to say it. "What a friend we have in Jesus." Start with Him. He is a friend that sticketh closer than a brother. Tell Him and others how much you love and appreciate them. "A friend loves at all times."

" 'That all of them may be one, Father, just as you are in me and I am in you. May they also be in us so that the world may believe that you have sent me.' "

John 17:21

This is a portion of the prayer of Jesus. Everyone of us should do our part in bringing it to pass. He said, "Love one another as I have loved you."

"All the believers were one in heart and mind. No one claimed that any of his possessions was his own, but they shared everything they had."

Acts 4:32

Genuine Christianity always makes its appearance in the form of great love and compassion for others. "The greatest of these is love."

"If I give all I possess to the poor and surrender my body to the flames, but have not love, I gain nothing."

1 Corinthians 13:3

God sees the heart behind the hand and the motive behind the gift.

" 'I am the bread of life.' "

John 6:48

In an age of miracles and mechanism, it is a sad report that half of the world goes to bed with empty stomachs because the other half retires with empty hearts.

"And this is love: that we walk in obedience to his commands . . ."

2 John 6

A shallow Christian will walk after his own desires, but love will prompt a person to "walk after his commandments." Follow the leader and always make sure that the leader is Christ.

"We know that we have passed from death to life, because we love our brothers. Anyone who does not love remains in death."

1 John 3:14

One of the big signs of the new birth is how we feel about other believers in Christ, irregardless of their church.

"Do not seek revenge or bear a grudge against one of your people, but love your neighbor as yourself. I am the Lord."

Leviticus 19:18

Lack of love has been the undoing of humanity.

———————

" 'For God so loved the world that he gave his one and only Son, that whoever believes in him shall not perish but have eternal life.' "

John 3:16

God's love is big enough to cover the world and, yet, individual enough so that the least of us are included.

———————

" 'My command is this: Love each other as I have loved you.' "

John 15:12

All the world's problems through Jesus will be settled at this point or not at all. "Now these three remain: faith, hope and love. But the greatest of these is love."

———————

"But God demonstrates his own love for us in this: While we were still sinners, Christ died for us."

Romans 5:8

It is not until we see ourselves as sinners that we can get a glimpse of the love of God, who sent Christ to die for the best and the worst of us. "This is love: not that we loved God, but that he loved us and sent his Son . . ."

———————

"I love you, O Lord, my strength."

Psalm 18:1

If the love of God is in our hearts, we will show it in our lives. "By this all men will know that you are my disciples, if you love one another."

———————

"Hatred stirs up dissension, but love covers over all wrongs."

Proverbs 10:12

The degree of our love for God is reflected in our willingness to forgive our fellow man. Love covers a lot of sin and reflects a great deal more spirit.

———————

" 'Why do you look at the speck of sawdust in your brother's eye and pay no attention to the plank in your own eye?' "

Matthew 7:3

Our vision always seems at its best when we are looking at another's faults. Oh God, give us good "insight" so that we can be understanding of others. In Jesus' name. Amen.

"For where you have envy and selfish ambition, there you find disorder and every evil practice."

James 3:16

It is so true. These two things open the door to a runaway of everything that is ungodly and unwholesome for a life or a nation. Only God can close the door and bring harmony and peace. "Love one another."

" 'If you love those who love you, what reward will you get? Are not even the tax collectors doing that?' "

Matthew 5:46

True Christianity makes a difference and will be demonstrated in "down to earth" works and "Christ-like" love.

"We know that we have passed from death to life, because we love our brothers. Anyone who does not love remains in death."

1 John 3:14

Behold the evidence of the changed life. Say it with love. "By this shall all men know that you are my disciples . . ."

"And now these three remain: faith, hope and love. But the greatest of these is love."

1 Corinthians 13:13

Love is the greatest force on earth and the prescription for the good life. Why don't we take it in and give it out?

Obedience to
God....

Obedience to God

"May the words of my mouth and the meditation of my heart be pleasing in your sight, O Lord, my Rock and my Redeemer."

Psalm 19:14

Not only what we talk about, but what we think about is screened by the Lord. Is it acceptable to the Lord?

_____

" 'I am grieved that I have made Saul king, because he has turned away from me and has not carried out my instructions.' Samuel was troubled, and he cried out to the Lord all that night."

1 Samuel 15:11

Saul's problem is a common one. He thought his "overall performance" was good enough to see him through. All the while, God was placing the emphasis on obedience to specific directives. God has not changed. "To obey is better than sacrifice."

_____

"I am the God of Bethel, where you anointed a pillar and where you made a vow to me. Now leave this land at once and go back to your native land."

Genesis 31:13

God has a running account of our kept and forgotten vows, and so often as the occasion arises, He calls for their fulfillment.

"Then the Lord told me, 'Go down from here at once, because your people whom you brought out of Egypt have become corrupt. They have turned away quickly from what I commanded them and have made a cast idol for themselves.' "

Deuteronomy 9:12

Humanity has not changed. When we lose touch with the true and living God, we start making our own. "Thou shalt worship the Lord thy God, and him only shalt thou serve."

" 'But when he, the Spirit of truth, comes, he will guide you into all truth. He will not speak on his own; he will speak only what he hears, and he will tell you what is yet to come.' "

John 16:13

One of our great problems is that we ask God for answers and guidance and then debate Him over His response. "Do whatever he tells you." "We must obey God."

"So whether you eat or drink or whatever you do, do it all for the glory of God."

1 Corinthians 10:31

Here is the argument settler. If you can't do a thing in accordance with His Word and will, don't do it. "Not my will, but yours, be done."

". . . 'We will do everything the Lord has said; we will obey.' "

Exodus 24:7

God's paths are clear. It is our dull hearing that gets us into trouble. "To obey is better than sacrifice." "We must obey God rather than men."

" 'But I gave them this command: Obey me, and I will be your God and you will be my people. Walk in all the ways I command you, that it may go well with you.' "

Jeremiah 7:23

Here is a condition and a promise that we cannot afford to ignore if we are to live happy and fruitful lives.

" 'Come, follow me,' Jesus said, 'and I will make you fishers of men.' "

Mark 1:17

Jesus beckons us to the world's greatest business. Only in eternity will we see just how great. Stop what you are doing and follow Jesus in this, the most rewarding work of all! "He who wins souls is wise."

"His master replied, 'Well done, good and faithful servant! You have been faithful with a few things; I will put you in charge of many things. Come and share your master's happiness!' "

Matthew 25:21

Contrary to what we sometimes think, we will be rewarded not for our success but on the basis of our faithfulness. "Be faithful, even to the point of death, and I will give you the crown of life."

"So the king gave the order, and they brought Daniel and threw him into the lions' den. The king said to Daniel, 'May your God, whom you serve continually, rescue you!' "

Daniel 6:16

Our job is dedication — His is deliverance. If we give attention to doing His will, the Lord is good enough to give us even beyond what we ask.

"If they obey and serve him, they will spend the rest of their days in prosperity and their years in contentment."

Job 36:11

Behold the emphasis on obedience and service! Looking for a success formula? Who can afford to overlook this one? Whatever the problem, He is the answer. Obey and follow Him.

"The Lord is my shepherd, I shall not be in want."

Psalm 23:1

The responsibility of caring for and leading belongs to the shepherd; the responsibility of obedience and following belongs to the sheep.

———————————

"We know that we have come to know him if we obey his commands."

1 John 2:3

The person who is well acquainted with the Lord will not be a stranger to His commandments.

———————————

"Everyone has heard about your obedience, so I am full of joy over you . . ."

Romans 16:19

Men who listen to what God has to say will usually have an audience to hear what they have to say. "To obey is better than sacrifice."

———————————

"If my people, who are called by my name, will humble themselves and pray and seek my face and turn from their wicked ways, then will I hear from heaven and will forgive their sin and will heal their land."

2 Chronicles 7:14

The crisis will pass when we meet God's conditions. "Call upon me in the day of trouble; I will deliver you, and you will honor me."

———————————

"He did what was right in the eyes of the Lord . . ."

2 Kings 15:34

If we major in what is right in God's sight, we don't have to worry about what it will look like in the eyes of man.

———————————

"The disciples went and did as Jesus had instructed them."

Matthew 21:6

The greatest need of the Church today is wholehearted obedience and down to earth preaching. "As the Father has sent me, I am sending you."

"Teach me to do your will . . ."

Psalm 143:10

The will of God will almost invariably be contrary to the ways of man. "For my thoughts are not your thoughts, neither are your ways my ways, declares the Lord."

"Blessed are those who wash their robes, that they may have the right to the tree of life and may go through the gates into the city."

Revelation 22:14

No man owns a part of that city until God owns all of that man.

" 'My sheep listen to my voice; I know them, and they follow me.' "

John 10:27

Father, we know that if You are mighty to save, then You can surely speak to us. Give us Your Divine directions today by Your spoken Word, and may we have obedience to follow, in Jesus' name. Amen.

"Love the Lord your God with all your heart and with all your soul and with all your strength."
Deuteronomy 6:5

God is not looking for a few shares in our life, but controlling interest. Nothing else will please Him — or us.

" 'No one can serve two masters. Either he will hate the one and love the other, or he will be devoted to the one and despise the other. You cannot serve both God and Money.' "
Matthew 6:24

It takes a sell-out to do business with God. "You shall have no other gods before me."

Our Every Need....

Our Every Need

"So do not throw away your confidence; it will be richly rewarded."

Hebrews 10:35

If you are hanging out there on a low limb, don't forget the One who made the tree. Look up, the Lord is waiting to give you a hand . . . and a new heart. Father, touch the ones who are struggling just now, and give them strength, in Jesus' name. Amen.

———————

"Ignoring what they said, Jesus told the synagogue ruler, 'Don't be afraid; just believe.' "

Mark 5:36

Fear not! Right now, if you invite Christ to take over your crisis, immediately you have all the power of Heaven in back of you. After the crisis, don't forget Him.

———————

" 'Again, I tell you that if two of you on earth agree about anything you ask for, it will be done for you by my Father in heaven.' "

Matthew 18:19

How simple! How Scriptural! Let's try it. Let's believe it. Think of a need that must be met. Whatever it may be, I will agree with you that it will be met now. In the name of Jesus and for the glory of God. Amen.

"The Lord works righteousness and justice for all the oppressed."

Psalm 103:6

Don't ever feel that the Lord is unaware of your burden. "He knows how we are formed." He knows the capacity of the load that we can carry and is standing by to shoulder it with us. "My help comes from the Lord."

"In Lystra there sat a man crippled in his feet, who was lame from birth and had never walked. He listened to Paul as he was speaking. Paul looked directly at him, saw that he had faith to be healed and called out, 'Stand up on your feet!' At that, the man jumped up and began to walk."

Acts 14:8-10

As long as there are men with needs, there will be a God of miracles to meet them. "I the Lord do not change." "Jesus Christ is the same yesterday and today and forever."

" 'Until now you have not asked for anything in my name. Ask and you will receive, and your joy will be complete.' "

John 16:24

Don't think you can ever overdraw the account of your Heavenly Father. "And my God will meet all your needs according to his glorious riches in Christ Jesus."

". . . for I am the Lord, who heals you."

Exodus 15:26

The healing from God covers the whole range of man from his soul and mind to his body . . . even to his material need! ". . . God does not show favoritism . . ." Whatever He has done for others, He can do it again for you. "I the Lord do not change." Holy Spirit, touch the need of this reader in the name of Jesus and for the glory of God. Amen.

"And we know that in all things God works for the good of those who love him, who have been called according to his purpose."

Romans 8:28

God is working on it! . . . and for our good. Don't take it upon yourself to give Him a time schedule or suggest the tools He is to use to get the job done.

———————————

"Cast all your anxiety on him because he cares for you."

1 Peter 5:7

The Lord has the answer to every problem of life, and the thing that really counts is that He cares.

———————————

" 'Leave here, turn eastward and hide in the Kerith Ravine, east of the Jordan. You will drink from the brook, and I have ordered the ravens to feed you there.' "

1 Kings 17:3, 4

On the authority of God's Word, needs can be met by means that will stagger the imagination of man. God can do anything, and today, you can believe Him for a miracle in your life.

———————————

" 'But seek first his kingdom and his righteousness and all these things will be given to you as well.' "

Matthew 6:33

Once we make Jesus the final authority in our lives, everything else becomes automatic. Let's pray, "Today we accept You as Saviour, and make You Lord. Amen."

———————————

" 'Sir,' the invalid replied, 'I have no one to help me into the pool when the water is stirred. While I am trying to get in, someone else goes down ahead of me.' Then Jesus said to him, 'Get up! Pick up your mat and walk.' "

John 5:7, 8

This is a story of a man who allowed Jesus to come into his life and exchange his explanation into an experience that put him on his feet. If you are looking for a real happening in your life, He is the one who can do it.

———————————

" 'For nothing is impossible with God.' "

Luke 1:37

This is the way God sees your problem. Turn what faith you have loose in the middle of this great promise and go on to victory. Father, I look to Your Word, and I pray that You will meet the need of this reader, no matter how hopeless it may appear, in the name of Jesus. Amen and thank You.

———————————

"So that your trust may be in the Lord, I teach you today, even you. Have I not written thirty sayings for you, sayings of counsel and knowledge."

Proverbs 22:19, 20

Life's answers are lost to us because we keep leaning to our own understanding or taking the advice of those who are as much in the dark as we are. Read the Bible every day and apply it to your everyday need.

———————————

" '. . . only one thing is needed . . .' "

Luke 10:42

There is one thing that is truly necessary in life, and that is to have Christ. There are many things in this life that are out of reach, but here is man's greatest need within the reach of all.

———————————

"And my God will meet all your needs according to his glorious riches in Christ Jesus."

Philippians 4:19

The unclaimed fortunes of Heaven are waiting to be delivered on earth to people of big faith and great vision. "With God all things are possible."

––––––––––––

"Cast all your anxiety on him because he cares for you."

1 Peter 5:7

It was never meant for us to bear the burdens of life, but rather, to share them with Him who knows us so well. We live beneath our privileges and above our heads when we seek to carry on without Him.

––––––––––––

"About midnight Paul and Silas were praying and singing hymns to God, and the other prisoners were listening to them. Suddenly there was such a violent earthquake that the foundations of the prison were shaken. At once all the prison doors flew open, and everybody's chains came loose."

Acts 16:25, 26

In the darkest hour of your life, look for the midnight specialist, the Lord Jesus, to open doors and solve your problems.

―――――――――

" 'So I say to you: Ask and it will be given to you; seek and you will find; knock and the door will be opened to you.' "

Luke 11:9

There are no problems that will not surrender to persistent prayer. "Lord, teach us to pray."

―――――――――

" 'All that the Father gives me will come to me, and whoever comes to me I will never drive away.' "

John 6:37

Whoever you are, whatever your need, the solution will be found in the Saviour. No habit or hurt is too much for Him to heal. You have tried everything else. Why not try Him? "Whosoever will may come."

―――――――――

"For God did not give us a spirit of timidity, but a spirit of power, of love and of self-discipline."

2 Timothy 1:7

The average person is apt to spend more time with his fears than he does with his faith. Father, banish the tormenting fears that come upon us by the power of the Holy Spirit, in Jesus' name. Amen.

———————

"He sent forth his word and healed them; he rescued them from the grave."

Psalm 107:20

The Word of God is the Great Physician in the person of Jesus on a mission of mercy, healing and ministering to all the needs of all the world. Let Him!

———————

"I cry aloud to the Lord; I lift up my voice to the Lord for mercy. I pour out my complaint before him; before him I tell my trouble."

Psalm 142:1, 2

Forget all the formalities and just tell God how you feel. Nor do you need to keep checking to see whether or not you got through. "Surely the arm of the Lord is not too short to save, nor his ear too dull to hear." Jesus said, "You may ask me for anything in my name, and I will do it."

———————

"Jesus looked at them and said, 'With man this is impossible, but with God all things are possible.' "

Matthew 19:26

If you are facing a situation and there is no way out, look up. Ask Him for proof; seek Him for power; apply this word to your worry. ". . . You do not have, because you do not ask God." Father, meet our impossible needs with Your Almighty power. In Jesus' name. Amen.

———————

"I am the Lord, the God of all mankind. Is anything too hard for me?"

Jeremiah 32:27

Weigh your problem over against His promise . . . and believe for the answer! ". . . Everything is possible for him who believes." "All authority in heaven and on earth has been given to me."

———————

"Oh, the depth of the riches of the wisdom and knowledge of God! How unsearchable his judgments, and his paths beyond tracing out!"

Romans 11:33

With that kind of resource, isn't it regrettable that we continue to live with our problems? God knows everything and can do anything. Look to Him for the answer.

———————

"There was a violent earthquake, for an angel of the Lord came down from heaven and, going to the tomb, rolled back the stone and sat on it. His appearance was like lightning, and his clothes were white as snow. The guards were so afraid of him that they shook and became like dead men."

Matthew 28:2-4

The God who did all of this to raise Jesus from the dead can today lift you up and let you out of whatever is holding you back from a new and abundant life. Rise up in His name. Amen.

———————

"Remember how the Lord your God led you . . ."

Deuteronomy 8:2

A clear memory of God's past blessings will keep us from panic at the thought of present day problems. He is still the same and is up to any emergency that may come upon you.

"In my anguish I cried to the Lord, and he answered by setting me free."

Psalm 118:5

In his most distressing moment, the true believer can expect divine deliverance. "He will remain faithful . . ."

"God is our refuge and strength, and ever-present help in trouble."

Psalm 46:1

Life presents no problems that Christ cannot solve.

"And my God will meet all your needs according to his glorious riches in Christ Jesus."

Philippians 4:19

We have yet to see what our God can do, and what we can do with Him in us and with us.

" 'If that is how God clothes the grass of the field, which is here today, and tomorrow is thrown into the fire, how much more will he clothe you, O you of little faith!' "

Luke 12:28

Victory is ours when we remember how much we mean to God. We are products of the providence of a Heavenly Father, fully capable of meeting our earthly needs.

"And my God will meet all your needs according to his glorious riches in Christ Jesus."

Philippians 4:19

If you belong to God, you are entitled to what He has. He invites you to ask for it. "Ask me for anything you want."

"For the Lord God is a sun and shield; the Lord bestows favor and honor; no good thing does he withhold from those whose walk is blameless."

Psalm 84:11

God is for us having the good things. We need to get our priorities in order so that we can have them.

———————

". . . pray for each other so that you may be healed."

James 5:16

Pray this promise! Just now, think of what you have need of and then pray for others who have the same need. In the mighty name of Jesus, my Father, I pray for others and I believe. Amen.

———————

" 'The silver is mine and the gold is mine,' declares the Lord Almighty."

Haggai 2:8

"For every animal of the forest is mine, and the cattle on a thousand hills."

Psalm 50:10

We need to cease acting as though God is poor and that He is unaware of our needs and unable to meet them. "Dear friend, I pray that you may enjoy good health and that all may go well with you, even as your soul is getting along well."

" 'But seek first his kingdom and his righteousness, and all these things will be given to you as well.' "

Matthew 6:33

It seems as though Jesus is saying that once our priorities are in order, answers to our prayers will be automatic.

" 'Which of you, if his son asks for bread, will give him a stone? Or if he asks for a fish, will give him a snake? If you, then, though you are evil, know how to give good gifts to your children, how much more will your Father in heaven give good gifts to those who ask him!' "

Matthew 7:9-11

Our God who created us will surely do as much for us as we would for our children. With that in mind, believe Him for your miracle. "For nothing is impossible with God."

" 'Ask and it will be given to you; seek and you will find; knock and the door will be opened to you.' "

Matthew 7:7

Believe God for anything while believing Him for the best thing. Our Father, take this prayer, in Jesus' name, to bring about miracles that cannot be denied or ignored. Amen.

———————————

"Proclaim the power of God, whose majesty is over Israel, whose power is in the skies."

Psalm 68:34

Look for His strength in the clouds of your life, for it shall surely be there. "Never will I leave you; never will I forsake you." Father, be with those in great distress just now, and may they feel Your presence and know that You care and deliver them, in Jesus' name. Amen.

———————————

"When I said, 'My foot is slipping' your love, O Lord, supported me."

Psalm 94:18

He is that close, and He cares. He does rescue us and His mercy endureth forever.

———————————

"Before they call I will answer; while they are still speaking I will hear."

Isaiah 65:24

The Lord is always out in front of us. "He knows the thought and the intent of the heart." Because He wants the best for us, He proceeds to answer many times in advance of our calling. What a father! — What a Saviour!

———————————

"And my God will meet all your needs according to his glorious riches in Christ Jesus."

Philippians 4:19

He is Savior, supplier and soon coming King. Worship Him now. Father, I pray for every need of every reader. Perform miracles in every area of life that cannot be denied or ignored, in Jesus' name. Amen and thank You.

" 'Call to me and I will answer you and tell you great and unsearchable things you do not know.' "

Jeremiah 33:3

God can bring to pass any promise that He has made. In this moment, think of your greatest need and let's believe God for the answer. In Jesus' name, oh God, for Your glory and our good, answer our prayer. Amen. We praise You.

". . . The Lord gives you relief from suffering and turmoil and cruel bondage."

Isaiah 14:3

In a moment of time, He can make up for all the hard times. "Cast all your anxiety on him because he cares for you."

"Do not hide your face from me when I am in distress. Turn your ear to me; when I call, answer me quickly."

Psalm 102:2

Feel free to talk to God like that. He understands the language of desperation and He will deliver. I am praying that your prayer will be answered for His glory and your good. Amen.

"Then Jesus came to them and said, 'All authority in heaven and on earth has been given to me.' "

Matthew 28:18

The next time you think about your big problem, take another look at Him who has all power. Apply that power to the problem. No problem!

"He himself bore our sins in his body on the tree, so that we might die to sins and live for righteousness; by his wounds you have been healed."

1 Peter 2:24

Move out on faith, accept all He has accomplished, and receive all He has promised. He said, "Never will I leave you; never will I forsake you." Father, grant great miracles in all our lives as we apply simple faith against all our needs, in Jesus' name. Amen. Thank You.

" 'I am the Lord, the God of all mankind. Is anything too hard for me?' "

Jeremiah 32:27

Put your biggest problem up against this great promise of the Lord and watch it dissolve. Father, in Jesus' name, please meet this reader with a miracle right now I pray. Amen.

"He himself bore our sins in his body on the tree, so that we might die to sins and live for righteousness; by his wounds you have been healed."

1 Peter 2:24

Calvary truly covered it all. Why will we wait when so much is waiting for us? Whatever the problem, He is the answer.

" 'Do not be like them, for your Father knows what you need before you ask him.' "

Matthew 6:8

Take time to thank Him for the needs met upon request, but also for the many met without request. "And my God will meet all your needs according to his glorious riches in Christ Jesus."

———————

" 'Look at the birds of the air; they do not sow or reap or store away in barns, and yet your heavenly Father feeds them. Are you not much more valuable than they?' "

Matthew 6:26

The Lord calls us to bird watching to build up our faith. The lessons we learn will lift us up above our own circumstances and give us a greater appreciation and love for our Creator, who gave us life to enjoy, not endure. Thanks, Jesus for the illustration.

———————

"Teach me your way, O Lord, and I will walk in your truth; give me an undivided heart, that I may fear your name."

Psalm 86:11

God is interested in needs. Prayer is the way to get them met. When was the last time that you spent some time in prayer? "You may ask me for anything in my name, and I will do it."

_____

" 'Come to me, all you who are weary and burdened, and I will give you rest.' "

Matthew 11:28

Think of all the peace we forfeit because we will not act on this promise. Father, we come with our burdens and we believe You for miracles, in Jesus' name. Amen, and thank You.

_____

" 'I am the good shepherd. The good shepherd lays down his life for the sheep.' "

John 10:11

On the cross, Jesus identified Himself with every sin, struggle and crisis of life. In this moment, receive that as a cure for every problem and go free forever. Father, I ask for salvation for everyone and liberation from every hurt and habit that may be harassing them. In Jesus' name, Amen.

_____

Peace - Happiness - Joy....

Peace - Happiness - Joy

"And the way of peace they do not know."
Romans 3:17

Man is continuously reaching out for peace while leaving God out of his plans. ". . . and on earth peace to men . . ." is still accompanied only by the presence of Christ.

"Blessed are the people of whom this is true; blessed are the people whose God is the Lord."
Psalm 144:15

Here is where happiness is! Isn't it strange that we have searched for it in so many other things and places? Father, forgive us, in Jesus' name. Amen.

"But the fruit of the Spirit is . . . joy . . ."
Galatians 5:22

It is not where we are, or who we are, but what and whose we are that makes us joyful.

"Restore to me the joy of your salvation . . ."
Psalm 51:12

Do you have the same joy, peace, and compassion for others that once ruled your spirit? If not, then turn to Him who hath begun a good work in you and is able to revive that which you seemed to have lost. Nothing but sin can take away the Christian's joy.

———————

"Therefore, since we have been justified through faith, we have peace with God through our Lord Jesus Christ."

Romans 5:1

There is no real peace inside, outside of Christ. He gives the peace that passeth all understanding. Peace that the world cannot give or take away.

———————

"For to us a child is born, to us a son is given, and the government will be on his shoulders. And he will be called Wonderful Counselor, Mighty God, Everlasting Father, Prince of Peace."

Isaiah 9:6

In our search for peace, it seems that we have called in everyone but the real peace-maker. "My peace I give you." Perhaps we need to make peace with God before we can talk peace with man.

" 'Blessed are the peacemakers, for they will be called sons of God.' "

Matthew 5:9

In our anxiety for peace with man, let us not pass a still greater obligation — that of making peace with Our Maker.

"For what I received I passed on to you as of first importance: that Christ died for our sins according to the Scriptures."

1 Corinthians 15:3

We must acknowledge personally that He died for our sins, if we are to have any personal peace.

"Nehemiah said, 'Go and enjoy choice food and sweet drinks, and send some to those who have nothing prepared. This day is sacred to our Lord. Do not grieve, for the joy of the Lord is your strength.'"

Nehemiah 8:10

True happiness comes from knowing the Lord, and true strength comes from the knowledge that He is with you, in you, and for you. "Never will I leave you; never will I forsake you."

———————

"How happy your men must be! How happy your officials, who continually stand before you and hear your wisdom!"

1 Kings 10:8

Don't condemn the emotional Christians. Perhaps they have found a joy that belongs to us all, but which we have heretofore ignored or overlooked. God's people ought to be the happiest and the busiest people on earth.

———————

" 'I have told you this so that my joy may be in you and that your joy may be complete.' "

John 15:11

The Christianity that Jesus talked about and provided for called for His people to be overjoyed, not overbearing nor overburdened.

"Let the peace of Christ rule in your hearts, since as members of one body you were called to peace. And be thankful."

Colossians 3:15

There can be no peace in our hearts until we make up our minds to come to terms with God. "My peace I give you."

"I will give them a heart to know me, that I am the Lord. They will be my people, and I will be their God, for they will return to me with all their heart."

Jeremiah 24:7

There is no peace of mind without whole-hearted surrender. "If . . . you seek the Lord your God, you will find him if you look for him with all your heart and with all your soul."

" 'Peace I leave with you; my peace I give you. I do not give to you as the world gives. Do not let your hearts be troubled and do not be afraid.' "

John 14:27

The peace that counts is found at an altar of prayer, not at a table. Let's get back to the Bible . . . and God.

———————

"But godliness with contentment is great gain."

1 Timothy 6:6

Do you ever see people like that? Perhaps they have read this and believed it. Let's join them!

———————

"And through him to reconcile to himself all things, whether things on earth or things in heaven, by making peace through his blood, shed on the cross."

Colossians 1:20

Just as the price of peace for every war has been the shedding of blood — so with eternal peace for our salvation. It was paid for by the blood of Jesus Christ, God's only begotten Son.

———————————

"Now may the Lord of peace himself give you peace at all times and in every way. The Lord be with all of you."

2 Thessalonians 3:16

He is the Peacemaker and the Peace-keeper. Turn all of the conflicts of your life over to Him. "My peace I give you."

———————————

"Therefore, since we have been justified through faith, we have peace with God through our Lord Jesus Christ."

Romans 5:1

Think of it. Peace with God. Without that, everything else in the world is reduced to nothing. Jesus said, "My peace I give you." By all means, take it.

———————————

"Therefore, since we have been justified through faith, we have peace with God through our Lord Jesus Christ."

Romans 5:1

Do you have peace with God? In this moment through Jesus, you can. Take it by faith forever. Receive and rejoice!

———————

"You love righteousness and hate wickedness; therefore God, your God, has set you above your companions by anointing you with the oil of joy."

Psalm 45:7

Make it a point to love the good things of life. The Lord will make it a point to see that you are rewarded. "No good thing does he withhold from those whose walk is blameless."

———————

"On the evening of that first day of the week, when the disciples were together, with the doors locked for fear of the Jews, Jesus came and stood among them and said, 'Peace be with you!' "

John 20:19

In a world of strife, the Savior is still the Peacemaker. "My peace I give you. I do not give to you as the world gives. Do not let your hearts be troubled and do not be afraid." Father, give peace to every troubled heart just now, in Jesus' name, Amen.

"My heart is steadfast, O God, my heart is steadfast; I will sing and make music."

Psalm 57:7

It's a great day in our lives when our hearts are right with God and our minds are at peace. Out of this experience will come joy unspeakable. It can happen today as we invite the Prince of Peace in. "My peace I give you."

" 'I have told you these things, so that in me you may have peace. In this world you will have trouble. But take heart! I have overcome the world.' "

John 16:33

The Lord doesn't want us to be under the circumstances, but an overcomer with Him. "My grace is sufficient for you." Whatever the problem, He is the answer.

" 'Peace I leave with you; my peace I give you. I do not give to you as the world gives. Do not let your hearts be troubled and do not be afraid.' "

John 14:27

He gives the peace that passes all understanding that the world cannot give, neither can it take away. Why don't we receive it? Father, in Jesus' great name, we receive the peace that You have promised. We also pray for peace world-wide. Amen. Thank You.

"Yet I will rejoice in the Lord, I will be joyful in God my Savior."

Habakkuk 3:18

There are good times in God's service. He planned it that way. Give Him praise. "Rejoice in the Lord always. I will say it again: Rejoice!" Not only prayer but praise is mountain moving.

Praising God....

Praising God

"Praise the Lord. Praise God in his sanctuary; praise him in his mighty heavens."

Psalm 150:1

When was the last time you heard praise in the sanctuary — that is to God! Praise ye the Lord. "Let everything that has breath praise the Lord."

"Extol the Lord, O Jerusalem; praise your God, O Zion, for he strengthens the bars of your gates and blesses your people within you. He grants peace to your borders and satisfies you with the finest of wheat."

Psalm 147:12-14

There is a time to shorten our petitions and lengthen our praise. We live in such a time. Praise ye the Lord!

"He led you through the vast and dreadful desert, that thirsty and waterless land, with its venomous snakes and scorpions. He brought you water out of hard rock."

Deuteronomy 8:15

If you have been out there in the wilderness, don't forget the guide who led you through it. Praise God from whom all blessings flow. Father, we praise You.

"And they stayed continually at the temple, praising God."

Luke 24:53

It's still true that more time in the temple and less time for the temporal makes for victorious living. "I rejoiced with those who said to me, 'Let us go to the house of the Lord.' "

". . . honor him, for he is your lord."

Psalm 45:11

Only One deserves our worship. Only One is worthy of our worship. The praise life will wear out the self life. "If . . . you seek the Lord your God, you will find him if you look for him with all your heart and with all your soul."

"Sing to the Lord, praise his name; proclaim his salvation day after day."

Psalm 96:2

Don't let your religion be a weekend matter for a weekend religion is a weak one. But every day, by work and by life, show forth His salvation.

". . . rejoice in all the good things the Lord your God has given to you and your household."

Deuteronomy 26:11

Have you thought to thank Him recently? Do you feel that the good things which you enjoy are accidental and through some effort of your own? Who gives you the power and wisdom and strength to get gain? Acknowledge the hand of God in your life now that it may be well with you in the future. "Let every thing that has breath praise the Lord."

"Give thanks in all circumstances . . ."

1 Thessalonians 5:18

Ingratitude is one of the great sins of our day. Follow this prescription and see if the praise life won't wear down the self life. "Be thankful."

"Praise be to the Lord, to God our Savior, who daily bears our burdens.   *Selah*"

Psalm 68:19

Have you stopped petitioning God long enough to praise Him lately? Count your blessings — if you can!

"I rejoiced with those who said to me, 'Let us go to the house of the Lord.' "

Psalm 122:1

Do you go to church to get it over with or to become a part of it? Let the worship service become a personal experience and go forward in your faith.

"Give thanks to the Lord, for he is good; his love endures forever."

Psalm 107:1

Give Him thanks for what even seems to be reverses today. Tomorrow you may discover that in His wise providence, they were advancements. "In all things God works for the good of those who love him . . ."

"Speak to one another with psalms, hymns and spiritual songs. Sing and make music in your heart to the Lord."

Ephesians 5:19

There is a lot to be said about talking to yourself and then there is a great deal more to be said about talking to God. Every day will be a better one if we will do both.

"Praise be to the Lord, to God our Savior, who daily bears our burdens.   *Selah*"
Psalm 68:19

It is not right to give thanks once a year for blessings received every day. "Sing forth the glory of his name; make his praise glorious!"

"Give thanks to the Lord of lords: *His love endures forever.*"

Psalm 136:3

Prayer unlocks the door. Praise keeps it open. "Praise God from whom all blessings flow."

"Praise the Lord, for the Lord is good; sing praise to his name, for that is pleasant."

Psalm 135:3

Praise should be a definite part of our life every day. It probably would surprise us if we knew how much answered prayer depends on our attitude of praise to God. "Give thanks to him and praise his name."

"Praise the Lord. Sing to the Lord a new song, his praise in the assembly of the saints."

Psalm 149:1

There is not only power in prayer but in praise. Have you ever thanked Him for things that appear to be going against you as well as what seems to be going for you? "Give thanks in all circumstances, for this is God's will for you in Christ Jesus."

"Be not afraid, O land; be glad and rejoice. Surely the Lord has done great things."

Joel 2:21

So many times the victory is in the rejoicing rather than in the pleading. Thank Him in advance now; and acknowledge that He is able to do above and beyond what you can ask or think.

"One of them, when he saw he was healed, came back, praising God in a loud voice. He threw himself at Jesus' feet and thanked him — and he was a Samaritan."

Luke 17:15, 16

We all go to Him in prayer, but how many times do we return to Him in thanks? And we hear a lot about prayer lists, but when was the last time you heard of a praise list? It is a good thing to give thanks unto the Lord.

"Who redeems your life from the pit and crowns you with love and compassion."

Psalm 103:4

How about giving God a word of thanks for what He did that you didn't see? Thank You, Lord!

———————

"It is good to praise the Lord and make music to your name, O Most High."

Psalm 92:1

Not only in times of abundance but in times of trials and adversity, it is good to give thanks. "Give thanks in all circumstances, for this is God's will for you in Christ Jesus."

———————

"But may all who seek you rejoice and be glad in you; may those who love your salvation always say, 'The Lord be exalted!' "

Psalm 40:16

Let's get our priorities straight. Make big of God! Man was never meant to be exalted and God ignored. God will not share His glory with another.

———————

"Praise the Lord. Praise God in his sanctuary; praise him in his mighty heavens. Praise him for his acts of power; praise him for his surpassing greatness. Let everything that has breath praise the Lord. Praise the Lord."

Psalm 150:1, 2, 6

For a well-rounded devotional life to God, it is obvious from His Word that the life of praise to Him should have equal time with our prayer life.

———————————

"Praise be to the Lord, to God our Savior, who daily bears our burdens.   *Selah*"

Psalm 68:19

We are defeated the moment we allow ourselves to start listing our burdens instead of counting our blessings. Note too, this is a "daily" matter with God to bestow His benefits . . . it should also be a daily matter with us to praise Him. "Lord, we do praise you." "Bless the Lord, O my soul, and forget not all his benefits."

———————————

" 'That all of them may be one, Father, just as you are in me and I am in you. May they also be in us so that the world may believe that you have sent me.' "

John 17:21

Why don't we quit waving church labels and just worship the Lord? This is what Jesus prayed for long ago. He is the way, the truth and life — the answer, the difference, everything. Let's follow Him together.

"My mouth is filled with your praise, declaring your splendor all day long."

Psalm 71:8

If you have faced something that has not surrendered to prayer, try praising God for it. "I will always have hope; I will praise you more and more."

"Praise be to the Lord, the God of Israel, from everlasting to everlasting. Then all the people said 'Amen' and 'Praise the Lord.' "

1 Chronicles 16:36

It should . be the normal thing, not unusual, for all of us to so respond when we think of His goodness. Praise ye the Lord!

————————

"This is the day the Lord has made; let us rejoice and be glad in it."

Psalm 118:24

He has made the day. Praising Him for it makes it better! From the rising of the sun to the going down thereof, His praise shall continually be in my mouth.

————————

"Great is the Lord and most worthy of praise; his greatness no one can fathom."

Psalm 145:3

Once we start praising Him, we can never really stop because there is no end to His greatness and our reason to be grateful.

"Sing to the Lord with thanksgiving; make music to our God on the harp. He covers the sky with clouds; he supplies the earth with rain and makes grass grow on the hills. He provides food for the cattle and for the young ravens when they call."

Psalm 147:7-9

A lot of confusion as to what happened to our prayers would clear up if we could only give a little more time in praising God. "Praise the Lord." Father, I praise Thee for health and happiness, for family and friends, the joy of Your service, Your Word, Church and most of all, for salvation and the baptism of Your Spirit.

"With whom I once enjoyed sweet fellowship as we walked with the throng at the house of God."

Psalm 55:14

More time in God's house will bring about better times in our house.

"Give thanks in all circumstances, for this is God's will for you in Christ Jesus."

1 Thessalonians 5:18

No matter how you feel or how things look, go ahead and give Him thanks and expect a change. "It is good to praise the Lord."

"When you have eaten and are satisfied, praise the Lord your God for the good land he has given you."

Deuteronomy 8:10

Praise is the pause that refreshes. Take time to thank God for the food . . . millions would like to do it for you.

"But may all who seek you rejoice and be glad in you; may those who love your salvation always say, 'Let God be exalted!' "

Psalm 70:4

We must be careful to hate nothing but sin, and exalt none but God. Oh Lord, we praise Thee!

"I have swept away your offenses like a cloud, your sins like the morning mist. Return to me, for I have redeemed you."

Isaiah 44:22

Praise the Lord! A God who will do all of that is worthy of our attention and allegiance forever. Whatever the problem, He is the answer.

"About Joseph he said: 'May the Lord bless his land with the precious dew from heaven above and with the deep waters that lie below; with the best the sun brings forth and the finest the moon can yield.' "

Deuteronomy 33:13, 14

How often do we praise Him for life personally, and for the production of the land at our disposal. All the glory is due to Thy name, Our Father, and we praise You in Jesus' name. Amen.

"And you and the Levites and the aliens among you shall rejoice in all the good things the Lord your God has given to you and your household."

Deuteronomy 26:11

Have you set aside your want list long enough to run a praise inventory to detail the blessings of God on you and your household? God said this is a good thing to do.

"It is good to praise the Lord and make music to your name, O Most High."

Psalm 92:1

Be as anxious to praise Him as you are to petition Him. The Bible says it's a good thing. It is also the right thing. "Let everything that has breath praise the Lord."

"In that day you will say: 'Give thanks to the Lord, call on his name; make known among the nations what he has done, and proclaim that his name is exalted.'"

Isaiah 12:4

Praise Him for what He has done, and in advance for what you expect Him to do. What a volume of praise would rise today if for one moment we would thank Him for past blessings. I praise Thee, oh God. Praise Father, Son, and Holy Ghost. Amen.

———————————

Prayer....

Prayer

" 'Call to me and I will answer you and tell you great and unsearchable things you do not know.' "

Jeremiah 33:3

The world has yet to see in full what God is willing to do in response to prevailing prayer. "With God all things are possible."

"In your distress you called and I rescued you, I answered you out of a thundercloud; I tested you at the waters of Meribah.   ***Selah***"

Psalm 81:7

Hold up that petition for a moment. Remember, and be thankful for the prayers that He has answered in the past. May all our prayers be preceded by praise.

"In my distress I called to the Lord; I called out to my God. From his temple he heard my voice; my cry came to his ears."

2 Samuel 22:7

Much of life is taken with trying to be heard of man, while God in Heaven waits to give us a ready audience any time we lift our voice. "I sought the Lord, and he answered me."

———————————

"By faith in the name of Jesus, this man whom you see and know was made strong. It is Jesus' name and the faith that comes through him that has given this complete healing to him, as you can all see."

Acts 3:16

We must remember that it's in the authority of Jesus' name that we can expect answers to our prayers. "You may ask me for anything in my name, and I will do it."

———————————

" 'If you, then, though you are evil, know how to give good gifts to your children, how much more will your Father in heaven give good gifts to those who ask him!' "

Matthew 7:11

We should not only be courageous in our asking, but confident of His answer.

———————————

"Lord, they came to you in their distress; when you disciplined them, they could barely whisper a prayer."

Isaiah 26:16

Very often, it is true, that the only time we look to Christ is when we get in a corner. A few moments with the Lord will keep us from the anxious hours ahead.

———————

"For this reason I kneel before the Father."

Ephesians 3:14

More bowing of the knees means less bowing to the world. You can go all the way to the top on your knees. Prayer is priceless. "Pray continually."

———————

"Again he prayed, and the heavens gave rain, and the earth produced its crops."

James 5:18

The Lord hears us when we pray, but sometimes tests our sincerity by how often we pray. Don't give up, and God will never let you down.

———————

". . . God, who answered me in the day of my distress . . ."

Genesis 35:3

He is still in the prayer-answering business. Whatever your grounds for asking, remember you must be on praying ground. Pray hardest when it's hardest to pray.

———————

" 'Again, I tell you that if two of you on earth agree about anything you ask for, it will be done for you by my Father in heaven.' "

Matthew 18:19

All you need to have a successful prayer meeting is for two people to agree that God is able.

———————

"I urge you, brothers, by our Lord Jesus Christ and by the love of the Spirit, to join me in my struggle by praying to God for me."

Romans 15:30

Prayer is the greatest contribution that we can make to the life of another. "Brothers, pray for us."

———————

" 'For everyone who asks receives; he who seeks finds; and to him who knocks, the door will be opened.' "

Matthew 7:8

Here is a three-fold formula for a successful prayer life. The turning point of our lives is when we truly turn everything over to Him in prayer. Pray on! He will not fail thee.

" 'Come now, let us reason together,' says the Lord. 'Though your sins are like scarlet, they shall be as white as snow; though they are red as crimson, they shall be like wool.' "

Isaiah 1:18

More time should be spent in taking our sins to God instead of brooding over them. "If we confess our sins, he is faithful and just and will forgive us our sins."

" 'When my life was ebbing away, I remembered you, Lord, and my prayer rose to you, to your holy temple.' "

Jonah 2:7

Why is it that we so often wait until we get down and out before we look up? "Whoever comes to me I will never drive away."

———————

"Then Samuel said, 'Assemble all Israel at Mizpah and I will intercede with the Lord for you.'"

1 Samuel 7:5

In our busy petitions for ourselves, we should stop long enough to exercise the glorious privilege of praying for each other. "Pray for each other."

———————

"Therefore confess your sins to each other and pray for each other so that you may be healed. The prayer of a righteous man is powerful and effective."

James 5:16

It is good to be pulling for someone, but much better to be praying for them. Right now, take a moment to lift a prayer for someone. It could mean the difference in their life here and their future in the hereafter.

———————

" 'You may ask me for anything in my name, and I will do it.' "

John 14:14

It's all in the authority of His name and in the power of His might. If Jesus is your Saviour, you are a member of God's family and have a right to His fortune which is limitless. Ask big and believe!

———————————

" 'If you believe, you will receive whatever you ask for in prayer.' "

Matthew 21:22

Go up against your greatest problem with this simple prayer pattern and look for answers, for they are sure to come. Jesus said, "I will do it."

———————————

"About midnight Paul and Silas were praying and singing hymns to God, and the other prisoners were listening to them. Suddenly there was such a violent earthquake that the foundations of the prison were shaken. At once all the prison doors flew open, and everybody's chains came loose."

Acts 16:25, 26

He is still opening doors in response to simple faith and prevailing prayer. Let us remember prisoners in every part of the world and every walk of life.

———————————

" 'And I will do whatever you ask in my name, so that the Son may bring glory to the Father.' "

John 14:13

Here is a promise for the man who will be daring enough to believe that the Lord is able to do what He said. Turn your world around. Start now to take Him at His Word.

———————————

"In my alarm I said, 'I am cut off from your sight!' Yet you heard my cry for mercy when I called to you for help."

Psalm 31:22

Many times in our impatience, we all have felt that we were cut off from Heaven, only to discover that there was a time span we were unaware of . . . and the Lord was on the line all along doing it His way. Keep talking to God. Don't let anything break down the line of communication. You're getting through, and God is coming through!

———————————

"My heart says of you, 'Seek his face!' Your face, Lord, I will seek."

Psalm 27:8

A prayer life that will reach God and touch humanity calls for something a great deal more than a casual approach. "Wait for the Lord."

"Devote yourselves to prayer, being watchful and thankful."

Colossians 4:2

Our prayers should always be followed by anticipation and gratitude. "Whatever you ask for in prayer, believe that you have received it, and it will be yours."

" 'Watch and pray so that you will not fall into temptation. The spirit is willing, but the body is weak.' "

Mark 14:38

Lack of prayer leaves a person open to many suggestions and little spirit to face them. A man out of touch with God will find evil pretty close at hand.

". . . one of his disciples said to him, 'Lord, teach us to pray . . .' "

Luke 11:1

It would seem that the closer a man is to the Lord, the more he sees his need of prayer. Prayer is a personal inventory of our spiritual needs and a private audience with Him "who sticks closer than a brother."

———————

". . . Come up here, and I will show you what must take place after this."

Revelation 4:1

You can't live in the valley and see very far. Mountain-top experiences are for knee-bending Christians.

———————

"The woman came and knelt before him. 'Lord, help me!' she said."

Matthew 15:25

Keep looking up, and the Lord will never let you down. Prayer changes things.

———————

"So Jacob was left alone, and a man wrestled with him till daybreak . . . So Jacob called the place Peniel, saying, 'It is because I saw God face to face, and yet my life was spared.' "

Genesis 32:24, 30

No man spends a night before God without victory in the morning. Prayer changes things.

———————————

"Always giving thanks to God the Father for everything, in the name of our Lord Jesus Christ."

Ephesians 5:20

We are not only to pray in His name, but to give thanks in His name.

———————————

" 'But when you pray, go into your room, close the door and pray to your Father, who is unseen. Then your Father, who sees what is done in secret, will reward you.' "

Matthew 6:6

Every word that we speak is recorded. Every prayer that we pray is rewarded. God said, "Surely the arm of the Lord is not too short to save, nor his ear too dull to hear."

———————————

" 'Ask and it will be given to you; seek and you will find; knock and the door will be opened to you.' "

Matthew 7:7

Don't give up! Keep your petition with praise before God. I join with them, my Father, in Jesus' name, that their prayer will be answered in Your will and time and for their good and Your glory. Amen.

"This, then, is how you should pray: 'Our Father in heaven, hallowed be your name, your kingdom come, your will be done on earth as it is in heaven. Give us today our daily bread. Forgive us our debts, as we also have forgiven our debtors. And lead us not into temptation, but deliver us from the evil one.' "

Matthew 6:9-13

Don't try to analyze or sermonize on this prayer. Just gather up all your problems and simply, slowly, and reverently repeat it. Let it be a daily part of you. In it, you are going to God in the words and in the name of His Son. You are bound to get results.

"But the tax collector stood at a distance. He would not even look up to heaven, but beat his breast and said, 'God, have mercy on me, a sinner.' "

Luke 18:13

Here is the prayer that brings the peace. Pray it now! When we acknowledge to God what we are, He immediately shows us what He will do. Jesus said, "Whoever comes to me I will never drive away."

———————

" 'For if you forgive men when they sin against you, your heavenly Father will also forgive you. But if you do not forgive men their sins, your Father will not forgive your sins.' "

Matthew 6:14, 15

Could this be what has happened to some of our prayers? . . . lost between these two verses!

———————

"You will pray to him, and he will hear you, and you will fulfill your vows."

Job 22:27

What a privilege it is to be heard by the One who has the whole world in His hands. His ear is not heavy that it cannot hear. His hand is not shortened that it cannot save. Pray on. Believe only!

"Before they call I will answer; while they are still speaking I will hear."

Isaiah 65:24

A prayer thought seems to be as good as a prayer said. God is always out in front of us. Pray boldly, believe big. He is able. Take your family to church. Pray for God's servant. God will bless you.

"I love those who love me, and those who seek me find me."

Proverbs 8:17

What kind of priority does prayer have? "But seek first his kingdom and his righteousness, and all these things will be given to you as well."

" 'Then you will call, and the Lord will answer; you will cry for help, and he will say: Here am I. If you do away with the yoke of oppression, with the pointing finger and malicious talk.' "

Isaiah 58:9

Look at this tremendous and tender communication that we can have with the Father through Jesus Christ, His Son. Why don't we pray more?

———————

"When this had dawned on him, he went to the house of Mary the mother of John, also called Mark, where many people had gathered and were praying."

Acts 12:12

There is no meeting like a real prayer meeting. What a privilege to pray for one another. I want to pray for whatever is holding you back or getting you down. Oh my Father, if it is a habit or a hurt, a disease or a devil, or whatever is oppressing this reader today, I ask You to deliver them in complete victory in Jesus' name. Amen.

———————

"God said to Solomon, 'Since this is your heart's desire and you have not asked for wealth, riches or honor, nor for the death of your enemies, and since you have not asked for a long life but for wisdom and knowledge to govern my people over whom I have made you king, therefore wisdom and knowledge will be given you. And I will also give you wealth, riches and honor, such as no king who was before you ever had and none after you will have.' "

2 Chronicles 1:11, 12

All of this followed when Solomon simply asked of the Lord, "Give your servant a discerning heart." Perhaps our prayers should be as unselfish. Why don't we pray the same prayer?

_____

"If I had cherished sin in my heart, the Lord would not have listened."

Psalm 66:18

Could this be where all of our unanswered prayers are bogged down? We alone can clear the line. Until then, it may be that God has us on hold.

_____

Rebuking Satan....

Rebuking Satan

"Submit yourselves, then, to God. Resist the devil, and he will flee from you."

James 4:7

Speak up to the devil in the name of Jesus. "The one who is in you is greater than the one who is in the world." Jesus said, "I am with you always."

"Do not be afraid, for I am with you; I will bring your children from the east and gather you from the west."

Isaiah 43:5

To know that He is with us! Isn't that great? The further word is, "If God is for us, who can be against us?" Praise God! We win!

"Jesus returned to Galilee in the power of the Spirit, and news about him spread through the whole countryside. He taught in their synagogues, and everyone praised him."

Luke 4:14, 15

As with Jesus, so it is with us. After the struggle with the enemy, there is strength.

"The one who is in you is greater than the one who is in the world."

"Jesus replied, 'I tell you the truth, everyone who sins is a slave to sin.'"

John 8:34

Sin is a hard boss to work for. Long hours, broken hearts, worried minds, and a multitude of bitter memories are the products of the devil. "The wages of sin is death." Be no longer the servant of sin when there is complete release in Christ.

"Do not be overcome by evil, but overcome evil with good."

Romans 12:21

Evil has never been a match for goodness. To be an overcomer, you have to overcome a few things. Let the good in your life be so pronounced that if people speak ill of you, no one will believe them.

" 'Why are you sleeping?' he asked them. 'Get up and pray so that you will not fall into temptation.' "

Luke 22:46

People need to be wide-awake and Spirit-filled, and then use common sense to avoid the snares of the devil.

"Then they got rid of the foreign gods among them and served the Lord . . ."

Judges 10:16

There are a lot of old and strange gods waiting in the shadows of our lives in search of new subjects. They leave only when the true and living God is given the place of prominence in our hearts.

"For the wages of sin is death, but the gift of God is eternal life in Christ Jesus our Lord."

Romans 6:23

Sin pays off . . . in bitter memories, heartache, shame, lost lives and souls. Christ is the way back and up. Jesus said, "I am the way and the truth and the life. No one comes to the Father except through me."

"You, dear children, are from God and have overcome them, because the one who is in you is greater than the one who is in the world."

1 John 4:4

We come to master the problems from without when we learn to appropriate power from within. "Nothing will be impossible for you."

―――――――――

"For everyone born of God overcomes the world. This is the victory that has overcome the world, even our faith."

1 John 5:4

The need of the hour is for more overcoming Christians with a song and fewer overbearing ones with a sigh.

―――――――――

"My son, if sinners entice you, do not give in to them."

Proverbs 1:10

Say "no" to sin, and the Lord will give you the strength to stand by your decision.

"The one who is in you is greater than the one who is in the world."

———————————

"Jesus said to him, 'Away from me, Satan! For it is written: "Worship the Lord your God, and serve him only." ' Then the devil left him, and angels came and attended him."

Matthew 4:10, 11

There is a liberation of our spirit that comes only from looking up to the Lord and speaking up to the devil. Resist the devil and he will flee from you. We overcome by the word of our testimony and the blood of the Lamb. Thank you, Lord, for the power of Your blood and the might of Your Word! Amen.

———————————

"Do not be overcome by evil, but overcome evil with good."

Romans 12:21

Keep firing away with good. Someday evil will surrender. "A gentle answer turns away wrath."

———————————

"Put on the full armor of God so that you can take your stand against the devil's schemes."

Ephesians 6:11

A Christian must fortify himself with the Word of God, exercise his faith, and walk in the Spirit. All of this is made easy with the one simple act of allowing Jesus His rightful place in our lives. "The one who is in you is greater than the one who is in the world."

"Be self-controlled and alert. Your enemy the devil prowls around like a roaring lion looking for someone to devour."

1 Peter 5:8

He is out there to devour your time, talents, your home, heart and eternal soul. The only language he understands is our true commitment to Jesus Christ. Today, make that commitment and walk on in confidence. "I am with you always."

"The God of peace will soon crush Satan under your feet. The grace of our Lord Jesus be with you."

Romans 16:20

Take this as your own promise of the power of God soon to be demonstrated in your life. "The one who is in you is greater than the one who is in the world."

"Submit yourselves, then, to God. Resist the devil, and he will flee from you."

James 4:7

With the resistance will come the release. The power of Jesus breaks the bondage of sin. "The Lord knows how to rescue godly men from trials."

Salvation....

Salvation

"Jesus answered, 'I am the way and the truth and the life. No one comes to the Father except through me.' "

John 14:6

Here is the way to God! Why go on without Him? The plan of salvation is simple, but must be taken seriously now.

"Salvation is found in no one else, for there is no other name under heaven given to men by which we must be saved."

Acts 4:12

Contrary to what so many seem to believe, salvation is in neither the church nor a cause, but through Christ alone. Jesus said, "I am the way."

"And he said: 'I tell you the truth, unless you change and become like little children, you will never enter the kingdom of heaven.' "

Matthew 18:3

Conversion is something more than surrounding your life with good works, religious thought and practice, or even the vain attempt to keep the law. It is a surrender of your will and way and a submission to the complete takeover by Christ.

"Here I am! I stand at the door and knock. If anyone hears my voice and opens the door, I will come in and eat with him, and he with me."

Revelation 3:20

What if suddenly you felt the silence of the departure of His presence, never to return again? "My Spirit will not contend with man forever." Answer the door now, and invite Him into the living room, the place where you live, and let Him take over for life.

"Salvation is found in no one else, for there is no other name under heaven given to men by which we must be saved."

Acts 4:12

Christ is the only door to eternal life and only unbelief can close it. "Believe in the Lord Jesus, and you will be saved."

"But if we walk in the light, as he is in the light, we have fellowship with one another, and the blood of Jesus, his Son, purifies us from all sin."

1 John 1:7

There is no blot on your life that can't be cleansed by the blood of Jesus Christ. Believe it and go free. "Though your sins are like scarlet, they shall be as white as snow."

"If we confess our sins, he is faithful and just and will forgive us our sins and purify us from all unrighteousness."

1 John 1:9

The man who fails to admit that he is a sinner is certain never to be saved. "All have sinned and come short of the glory of God."

" 'I am the gate; whoever enters through me will be saved. He will come in and go out, and find pasture.' "

John 10:9

Pity the man who finally closes the door in his own face by his failure to take God at His Word. When He closes the door, no man can open it. When He opens it, no man can close it.

———————————

"And everyone who calls on the name of the Lord will be saved."

Acts 2:21

God has no favorites. He is no respecter of persons. No sin is too great, no sinner so vile but what He will forgive.

———————————

"May I never boast except in the cross of our Lord Jesus Christ . . ."

Galatians 6:14

The cross is a constant reminder that we are helpless in the saving of our own souls. It was Christ who died and rose again to put eternal hope within reach of all.

———————————

"For all have sinned and fall short of the glory of God."

Romans 3:23

No sinner is so bad but what he can find refuge in the goodness of God through Christ the Saviour. "Jesus saves."

———————

"Repent, then, and turn to God, so that your sins may be wiped out, that times of refreshing may come from the Lord."

Acts 3:19

It takes more than a good thought or a kind act to assure a man of eternal life. Our salvation cost Jesus Christ His life, and it will cost us at least our pride in acknowledging that He did it for us.

———————

"I have swept away your offenses like a cloud, your sins like the morning mist. Return to me, for I have redeemed you."

Isaiah 44:22

Many times the Lord is far more willing to forgive our sins than we are to forget them. "So if the Son sets you free, you will be free indeed."

"For he says, 'In the time of my favor I heard you, and in the day of salvation I helped you.' I tell you, now is the time of God's favor, now is the day of salvation."

2 Corinthians 6:2

Your eternal salvation is too important to put off until a day that you may never see. "Choose for yourselves this day whom you will serve."

———————

"Instead, you ought to say, 'If it is the Lord's will, we will live and do this or that.' "

James 4:15

Perhaps it's all right to plan for tomorrow so long as you keep in mind who provides for it. Too many of man's plans have been left on the drawing board because God was left out. Today is the day of salvation. Make everything else secondary to this.

———————

"For it is by grace you have been saved, through faith — and this not from yourselves, it is the gift of God — not by works, so that no one can boast."

Ephesians 2:8, 9

There is absolutely nothing that you can do to bring about your salvation apart from freely accepting what Jesus has already done. Make no mistake about it, however, there is work to be done after salvation. Work while it is day. The night cometh when no man can work.

———————

" 'I tell you, no! But unless you repent, you too will all perish.' "

Luke 13:3

Jesus was talking to well-disciplined, well-churched, well-read, but all was not well inside because they had not turned from their sins. Repentance is turning around, not slowing down, or standing still. The man who would be saved must do something with Jesus Christ, and then he must do something for Him.

———————

"I have swept away your offenses like a cloud, your sins like the morning mist. Return to me, for I have redeemed you."

Isaiah 44:22

In the process of His cleansing, the Saviour never leaves a stain.

"Thanks be to God for his indescribable gift!"

2 Corinthians 9:15

So many have failed to acknowledge the gift, much less thank Him for it. "The gift of God is eternal life in Jesus Christ our Lord."

"For it is by grace you have been saved, through faith — and this is not from yourselves, it is the gift of God — not by works, so that no one can boast."

Ephesians 2:8, 9

No man is good enough to save himself, and no man is so bad that God will not do it for him. Christ died for our sins. "Though your sins are like scarlet, they shall be as white as snow."

"If we confess our sins, he is faithful and just and will forgive us our sins and purify us from all unrighteousness."

1 John 1:9

It is as we unburden ourselves to the Lord that He unveils His forgiveness to us. He said, "I will forgive their wickedness and will remember their sins no more." Believe it now, be happy forever.

———————————

"For all have sinned and fall short of the glory of God."

Romans 3:23

The whole world is guilty before God and is up for penalty or pardon, and every man must decide for himself which it will be. The Lord is waiting for your decision now. "Jesus saves."

———————————

"So then, each of us will give an account of himself to God."

Romans 14:12

Every man's record is waiting for him at the end of life's day. Old accounts are settled on earth or faced in eternity. Your Heavenly Father will forgive you in Jesus' name.

"For the message of the cross is foolishness to those who are perishing, but to us who are being saved it is the power of God."
1 Corinthians 1:18

Take the cross out of the Christian message and we have nothing to say to the world or any solution for our sins. "Christ died for our sins."

"If we claim we have not sinned, we make him out to be a liar and his word has no place in our lives."
1 John 1:10

If we refuse to see ourselves as sinners, we place ourselves outside the reach of the Saviour. He came not to call the righteous but sinners to repentance.

"They went out and preached that people should repent."

Mark 6:12

This may not be the most popular message, but no one can deny that it is the most needed. Repentance is turning our backs on the old life and our hearts over to a New Leader.

————————

"For it is by grace you have been saved, through faith — and this not from yourselves, it is the gift of God."

Ephesians 2:8

No amount of work can save you, but just a little faith will write your name in the Book of Life. Scrap your plans and accept His plan of salvation.

————————

"And I saw the dead, great and small, standing before the throne, and books were opened. Another book was opened, which is the book of life. The dead were judged according to what they had done as recorded in the books."

Revelation 20:12

Only on this side of the grave can you settle the old account. Don't leave it hanging. It will follow you into judgment. You can know now about the future. "He that believes in the Son has everlasting life."

―――――――――

" 'I tell you the truth, whoever hears my word and believes him who sent me has eternal life and will not be condemned; he has crossed over from death to life.' "

John 5:24

In an hour when the magic word is transplant, don't lose sight of the Great Physician's ability to transform. One stretches out the old life on earth. The other assures eternal life in Heaven. "If anyone is in Christ, he is a new creation."

―――――――――

"That if you confess with your mouth, 'Jesus is Lord,' and believe in your heart that God raised him from the dead, you will be saved. For it is with your heart that you believe and are justified, and it is with your mouth that you confess and are saved."

Romans 10:9, 10

The person who really believes in his heart ought to have a bold testimony to go with it. "Let the redeemed of the Lord say this."

———————

"For everyone born of God overcomes the world. This is the victory that has overcome the world, even our faith."

1 John 5:4

Most of us surrender in one way or the other to the call of the world, when all the while, as Christians, we are called to be overcomers. "They overcame him by the blood of the Lamb and by the word of their testimony."

———————

"But if we walk in the light, as he is in the light, we have fellowship with one another, and the blood of Jesus, his Son, purifies us from all sin."

1 John 1:7

No sin is beyond the cleansing blood of Jesus when we simply come to Him in simple faith, believing. "Christ died for our sins."

———————

"All of us have become like one who is unclean, and all our righteous acts are like filthy rags; we all shrivel up like a leaf, and like the wind our sins sweep us away."

Isaiah 64:6

Don't rely on your righteousness to save you. Outside of Christ, there is no chance. Jesus said . . . "I am the way and the truth and the life; no one comes to the Father except through Me."

———————————

"I said, 'O Lord, have mercy on me; heal me, for I have sinned against you.' "

Psalm 41:4

Every man's soul very often stands in need of spiritual repair. The Great Physician, Christ Jesus, stands ready to do the job. He has never lost a patient.

———————————

"For Christ died for sins once for all, the righteous for the unrighteous, to bring you to God. He was put to death in the body but made alive by the Spirit."

1 Peter 3:18

Why continue to live with sin that Jesus has already died for? Whether you understand it or not, believe it and go free. It is our responsibility to acknowledge our need and His to meet it. This He has already done. Count it as so. Father, we admit that we are sinners and that we cannot save ourselves. However, we acknowledge that Jesus is the Saviour, and we accept Him now in His name. Amen.

———————

". . . be sure that your sin will find you out."

Numbers 32:23

———————

Sin, unforgiven by the Lord, is a dangerous thing to have on the loose. Under the blood of Christ, however, sin has lost its dread and power. He will forgive.

———————

"Jesus straightened up and asked her, 'Woman, where are they? Has no one condemned you?' 'No one, sir,' she said. 'Then neither do I condemn you,' Jesus declared. 'Go now and leave your life of sin.' "

John 8:10, 11

People who dangle a past before a person ought to be conscious of the Lord's presence. "But if you do not forgive men their sins, your Father will not forgive your sins."

" 'That everyone who believes in him may have eternal life.' "

John 3:15

Our future in the hereafter is decided in the here and now. "Now is the day of salvation."

". . . our salvation is nearer now than when we first believed. The night is nearly over; the day is almost here . . ."

Romans 13:11, 12

Every day brings us closer to the eventual meeting with God. Will it be reward or wrath? Only you can decide that.

"For all have sinned and fall short of the glory of God."

Romans 3:23

Sin is so common, but, thank God, forgiveness is so close. Jesus said, "Whoever comes to me I will never drive away."

"But if we walk in the light, as he is in the light, we have fellowship with one another, and the blood of Jesus, his Son, purifies us from all sin."

1 John 1:7

Take a good look at the word "all." There will be times when you will need to remember how deep the cleansing and how much he cares. "He cares for you."

"That if you confess with your mouth, 'Jesus is Lord,' and believe in your heart that God raised him from the dead, you will be saved. For it is with your heart that you believe and are justified, and it is with your mouth that you confess and are saved."

Romans 10:9-10

Salvation is a matter of repentance, believing, and receiving. It should be followed by a lot of sharing.

"For Christ died for sins once for all, the righteous for the unrighteous, to bring you to God. He was put to death in the body but made alive by the Spirit."

1 Peter 3:18

Calvary was a one-time sacrifice for our all-time deliverance.

"Then he adds: 'Their sins and lawless acts I will remember no more.'"

Hebrews 10:17

Talk to the Lord about your sin problem; ask Him for Jesus' sake to forgive you; and then forget it as He does. How can you remember something that no longer exists? Jesus said, "Go in peace and be freed from your suffering."

"Salvation is found in no one else, for there is no other name under heaven given to men by which we must be saved."

Acts 4:12

It's all in the name of Jesus! To introduce anyone or anything as a substitute or as a means for our salvation is to say that God made a mistake and the death of Jesus was without purpose. In Him is life.

———————

"That if you confess with your mouth, 'Jesus is Lord,' and believe in your heart that God raised him from the dead, you will be saved. For it is with your heart that you believe and are justified, and it is with your mouth that you confess and are saved."

Romans 10:9, 10

Obey the scripture; read it slowly; and be saved forever. The Christian life consists of believing, receiving and sharing. For a truly happy and productive life, take Him into your heart at once and tell it as often as you can! "You are my witnesses."

———————

"As far as the east is from the west, so far has he removed our transgressions from us."

Psalm 103:12

Don't be looking for your past sins; in Christ they are far removed. Just be glad that they are. Father, thank You so much for forgiveness for the past, the privilege of the present and the promise of Your guidance and presence for the future. In Jesus' name. Amen.

———————

" 'All that the Father gives me will come to me, and whoever comes to me I will never drive away.' "

John 6:37

Cheer up! There is no small print in His great promise. If you have ever had any doubt that He would receive you, read this again and go to Him at once. He loves you. Attend the services in your church . . . feel better all week.

———————

"They replied, 'Believe in the Lord Jesus, and you will be saved — you and your household.' "

Acts 16:31

Take this simple message of release and reality, without alteration or addition, to as many people as you can find, and let the Holy Spirit do the rest. "Come . . . and I will give you rest."

———————

"When he came to his senses, he said, 'How many of my father's hired men have food to spare, and here I am starving to death! I will set out and go back to my father and say to him: Father, I have sinned against heaven and against you.' "

Luke 15:17, 18

It's a great day in a man's life when he finally wakes up to where he is and what he is missing at the Father's house. Your Heavenly Father will forgive you. In Jesus' name, He will!

———————

" 'Whoever believes in him is not condemned, but whoever does not believe stands condemned already because he has not believed in the name of God's one and only Son.' "

John 3:18

Salvation is not a wait-and-see; it is already settled for the believer . . . and the unbeliever. The only way to lift the condemnation is to accept Christ.

———————

"If we confess our sins, he is faithful and just and will forgive us our sins and purify us from all unrighteousness."

1 John 1:9

We have too many "nicknames" for sins. We need to call them as God sees them, acknowledge them before Him, and ask Jesus to cover them with His blood. The blood of Jesus Christ, God's Son, cleanseth us from all sin.

———————

"Finally Pilate handed him over to them to be crucified. So the soldiers took charge of Jesus. Carrying his own cross, he went out to the place of the Skull (which in Aramaic is called Golgotha). Here they crucified him, and with him two others — one on each side and Jesus in the middle."

John 19:16-18

Here is where the price was paid for our pardon, but everyone of us individually must acknowledge it was our sin that caused it before the pardon is valid. "Christ died for our sins."

"Then he said, 'Jesus, remember me when you come into your kingdom.' "

Luke 23:42

The man who makes reservations in this life will have no regrets in the life to come.

"You have set our iniquities before you, our secret sins in the light of your presence."

Psalm 90:8

The beauty of it all is that the One who sees us as we are is willing to make us what we ought to be. In Jesus' name He will. "Whoever comes to me I will never drive away."

". . . 'Repent, for the kingdom of heaven is near.' "

Matthew 3:2

Repentance is turning around and "coming to." "Come to me, all you who are weary and burdened, and I will give you rest."

———————

"For it is by grace you have been saved, through faith — and this not from yourselves, it is the gift of God — not by works, so that no one can boast."

Ephesians 2:8, 9

No man works his way up to Heaven. Our eternal salvation is settled in the Saviour, not in the efforts of man.

———————

"For there is one God and one mediator between God and men, the man Christ Jesus."

1 Timothy 2:5

We are saved by the grace of God through the crucifixion of Christ. Man must accept God's plan or prepare for His punishment.

"If you confess with your mouth, 'Jesus is Lord,' and believe in your heart that God raised him from the dead, you will be saved."

Romans 10:9

The evidence of real Christian experience is a combination of what we feel in our hearts and what we say with our lives.

"The Lord is witness against you, and also his anointed is witness this day."

1 Samuel 12:5

The testimony of a crucified Saviour will condemn or release one and all in the hour of judgment. Your future can be settled now by accepting Him.

"Surely the arm of the Lord is not too short to save, nor his ear too dull to hear."

Isaiah 59:1

God is ever ready and ever merciful to hear the faintest cry and save the vilest sinner. God is love.

———————

". . . I tell you, now is the time of God's favor, now is the day of salvation."

2 Corinthians 6:2

A man's life on earth and his eternal welfare in the life to come hinges on a decision that he can make in one minute. Decide now; your whole destiny depends on it.

———————

"In reply Jesus declared, 'I tell you the truth, no one can see the kingdom of God unless he is born again.' "

John 3:3

It is impossible for man to have a new life without a new birth. Being a Christian is a great deal more than joining a church and making resolutions. It is experiencing a regeneration through a crucified Redeemer.

———————

"Therefore, there is now no condemnation for those who are in Christ Jesus."

Romans 8:1

The person who settles up with God here won't have to face an outstanding account in the life to come. "Believe on the Lord Jesus Christ and you will be saved."

"But God demonstrates his own life for us in this: While we were still sinners, Christ died for us."

Romans 5:8

Salvation is on a come-as-you-are basis, and people who consider themselves too good to be lost will never be saved. "All have sinned and come short of the glory of God."

" '. . . whoever comes to me I will never drive away.' "

John 6:37

Every honest seeker in Christ will find his eternal salvation. Nothing shall separate us from the love of God.

"If we confess our sins, he is faithful and just and will forgive us our sins and purify us from all unrighteousness."

1 John 1:9

It is as we unburden ourselves to the Lord that He unveils His forgiveness to us. He said, "I will remember their sins no more." Believe it now, be happy forever.

"Then Jesus said to her, 'Your sins are forgiven.' "

Luke 7:48

Man can excuse sin, but Jesus can forgive them. "If we confess our sins, he is faithful and just and will forgive us our sins and purify us from all unrighteousness."

"I, even I, am he who blots out your transgressions, for my own sake, and remembers your sins no more."

Isaiah 43:25

God does what very few people attempt to do; forget the sins of others.

"For all have sinned and fall short of the glory of God."

Romans 3:23

Even little sins can keep us from doing big things. Your Heavenly Father will forgive you for Christ's sake.

"Those who accepted his message were baptized, and about three thousand were added to their number that day. They devoted themselves to the apostles' teaching and to the fellowship, to the breaking of bread and to prayer."

Acts 2:41, 42

After the revival, they were still around rejoicing and reaching out for others. This is the evidence of repentance and regeneration.

" 'The time has come,' he said. 'The kingdom of God is near. Repent and believe the good news!' "

Mark 1:15

Nothing happens in the heart until the mind is changed. "I have considered my ways and have turned my steps to your statutes."

"Let the wicked forsake his way and the evil man his thoughts. Let him turn to the Lord, and he will have mercy on him, and to our God, for he will freely pardon."

Isaiah 55:7

Here is the road back and the reason for taking it. "Seek the Lord while he may be found; call upon him while he is near." "With you there is forgiveness." We praise thee, oh God.

"If we confess our sins, he is faithful and just and will forgive us our sins and purify us from all unrighteousness."

1 John 1:9

We must acknowledge our need if we want it met. Pretense only prolongs the agony . . . and besides that, it is a frightening risk to take. "My Spirit will not contend with man forever."

" 'Come to me, all you who are weary and burdened, and I will give you rest. Take my yoke upon you and learn from me, for I am gentle and humble in heart, and you will find rest for your souls. For my yoke is easy and my burden is light.' ."

Matthew 11:28-30

You can't beat this invitation, but it's not going to be there forever. Today is the day of Salvation. You will never relive today. Make it a good one with God's help.

———————

"On the last and greatest day of the Feast, Jesus stood and said in a loud voice, 'If anyone is thirsty, let him come to me and drink.' "

John 7:37

Only Christ knows the real longing of every life, and He alone can fill it. Why wander in the wilderness ignoring His invitation? "Come to me . . . I will give you rest."

———————

Serving God....

Serving God

"But you are a chosen people, a royal priesthood, a holy nation, a people belonging to God, that you may declare the praises of him who called you out of darkness into his wonderful light."

1 Peter 2:9

We are not redeemed by God just to enjoy our experience, but to share it. He is not looking for authorities, just witnesses. "Let the redeemed of the Lord say this."

———————————

"I rejoiced with those who said to me, 'Let us go to the house of the Lord.'"

Psalm 122:1

You can tell those who love the Lord by the excuses they find to attend His House. You can also tell those who don't love Him so much by the excuses they seem to find to stay away from His House. Christ loved the Church, and gave Himself for it.

———————————

"Whatever your hand finds to do, do it with all your might, for in the grave, where you are going, there is neither working nor planning nor knowledge nor wisdom."

Ecclesiastes 9:10

If more Christians would sincerely put their hands, hearts and heads in the work of the Lord, there would be such a change overnight that it would be hard for the world to recognize the Church.

"If you confess with your mouth, 'Jesus is Lord,' and believe in your heart that God raised him from the dead, you will be saved."

Romans 10:9

The surrendered Christian life is a combination of believing, trusting and telling. "Trust in the Lord with all your heart." "Go . . . tell them how much the Lord had done for you."

"But be sure to fear the Lord and serve him faithfully with all your heart; consider what great things he has done for you."

1 Samuel 12:24

God calls for a great deal more than a part time commitment and a casual approach to Christianity. Seek Him with your whole heart and ye shall find Him.

" 'He must become greater; I must become less.' "

John 3:30

The business of every Christian is to lift up the Saviour and play down self. The greatest problem of the Church is that we have not held Him up as the answer.

" 'I, Jesus, have sent my angel to give you this testimony for the churches. I am the Root and the Offspring of David, and the bright Morning Star.' "

Revelation 22:16

Jesus still has a message for the Church today to be delivered by men who will tell it like it is, so that we may no longer be as we are. Preach the Word!

" 'Therefore go and make disciples of all nations, baptizing them in the name of the Father and of the Son and of the Holy Spirit, and teaching them to obey everything I have commanded you. And surely I am with you always, to the very end of the age.' "

Matthew 28:19, 20

The average church is designed to suit and seat the people, and all the while God intended it as an instrument to send us! On with the message of love . . . we have been seated long enough.

"As you hold out the word of life — in order that I may boast on the day of Christ that I did not run or labor for nothing."

Philippians 2:16

Here's news, Christian friend. Our greatest job is not to explain the Word of God, but to extend it.

" 'You are the light of the world . . .' "

Matthew 5:14

Not just the Church, not a select few, but each one in his own way that stands for the cause of Christianity. How much light have you been responsible for to dispense the gloom and doubt of a troubled soul yet in darkness?

"The night is nearly over; the day is almost here. So let us put aside the deeds of darkness and put on the armor of light."

Romans 13:12

The person who has the light ought to be shining. Let your light so shine that men may see your good works and glorify your Father, which is in Heaven.

" 'As you sent me into the world, I have sent them into the world.' "

John 17:18

The job of every Christian is to continue the work of Christ through personal experience and public example. "You are my witnesses."

"He said to them, 'Go into all the world and preach the good news to all creation.' "

Mark 16:15

As we are straining to reach the moon, we are faced with the mounting evidence to suggest that we haven't reached the earth as yet.

". . . See to it that you complete the work you have received in the Lord."

Colossians 4:17

God has big jobs that can be filled with little people. He is no respecter of persons.

" 'But while everyone was sleeping, his enemy came and sowed weeds among the wheat, and went away.' "

Matthew 13:25

Christians ought to be wide awake and up and doing. "Night is coming."

"Remember your Creator in the days of your youth . . ."

Ecclesiastes 12:1

You can't give God what's left of life and expect His best. Give Him the best and the rest of your life.

———————

" 'If you love me, you will obey what I command.' "

John 14:15

The need of the hour is for more Christians to obey the Lord's Word and do His work. A good test of our love for God is in how much we trust His Word.

———————

"Surely the arm of the Lord is not too short to save, nor his ear too dull to hear."

Isaiah 59:1

Wherever you are, He can hear you and reach you. Therefore, reach out and take the extended hand of Christ, and then be His instrument to touch a lost and dying world.

———————

"Do you not say, 'Four months more and then the harvest?' I tell you, open your eyes and look at the fields! They are ripe for harvest."

John 4:35

The heart's cry of every Christian ought to be, "God give me a vision of what can be done and what must be done before it is too late." Work while it is day. The night cometh.

"For we cannot help speaking about what we have seen and heard."

Acts 4:20

If you find it difficult to speak for the Lord, consider the first Christians who said, "We cannot help speaking." The need seems to be for more of what they had. "God does not show favoritism."

" 'You are the salt of the earth. But if the salt loses its saltiness, how can it be made salty again? It is no longer good for anything, except to be thrown out and trampled by men.' "

Matthew 5:13

There are too many tasteless Christians who could use a little spiritual seasoning to sharpen their testimony, and at the same time, help put a good taste in the mouth of the world they see daily.

" 'Whoever acknowledges me before men, I will also acknowledge him before my Father in heaven.' "

Matthew 10:32

If you keep your salvation a secret here, don't expect such a royal reception in Heaven. "You are my witnesses."

"But the fruit of the Spirit is love, joy, peace, patience, kindness, goodness, faithfulness, gentleness and self-control. Against such things there is no law."

Galatians 5:22, 23

Not only the proclamation of Christianity, but the evidence of it, is important.

"For those God foreknew he also predestined to be conformed to the likeness of his Son, that he might be the firstborn among many brothers."

Romans 8:29

If the world can catch the image of Christ in believers, it shouldn't be long in making the conversion. "You are my witnesses."

" 'Therefore go and make disciples of all nations, baptizing them in the name of the Father and of the Son and of the Holy Spirit.' "

Matthew 28:19, 20

You will be glad in eternity that you did all that you could to evangelize the earth. Do it with all your love, might and means.

———————

" 'In the same way, any of you who does not give up everything he has cannot be my disciple.' "

Luke 14:33

God offers untold blessings for unconditional surrender. "But seek first his kingdom and his righteousness, and all these things will be given to you as well."

———————

" 'Take my yoke upon you and learn from me, for I am gentle and humble in heart, and you will find rest for your souls.' "

Matthew 11:29

The safest place and the sweetest place is to be in His will and at His service.

———————

" 'Behold, I am coming soon! My reward is with me, and I will give to everyone according to what he has done.' "

Revelation 22:12

"When the roll is called up yonder" we will be rewarded in accordance with what we have done down here. Work while it is day. The night cometh when no man can work.

———————

"As the body without the spirit is dead, so faith without deeds is dead."

James 2:26

The man who has faith ought to be anxious to prove that it is workable.

———————

" 'Be on guard! Be alert! You do not know when that time will come.' "

Mark 13:33

Time is in God's hands; talents are in our hands. We ought to use them wisely before time runs out. "The time is short."

" '. . . And who knows but that you have come to royal position for such a time as this?' "

Esther 4:14

God places us with a purpose, and He has never misplaced anyone.

"For we must all appear before the judgment seat of Christ, that each one may receive what is due him for the things done while in the body, whether good or bad."

2 Corinthians 5:10

Every Christian will be judged as to how seriously he took the work of Christ and the worth of a soul. Have you given your best to Jesus?

" '. . . worship the Lord your God, and serve him only.' "

Matthew 4:10

Strange and curious gods daily make their appearance in all of our lives to crowd out the true and living God. Let it be known that you are not for hire. It is a noble thing to be a real servant.

———————

" 'Whoever finds his life will lose it, and whoever loses his life for my sake will find it.' "
Matthew 10:39

Man truly finds himself in life as he loses himself in the will of the Lord. Make the investment of thyself in the work of God; there are no greater dividends.

———————

"Let us not become weary in doing good, for at the proper time we will reap a harvest if we do not give up."
Galatians 6:9

The man who majors in doing good will not have bad memories.

———————

"He told them, 'The harvest is plentiful, but the workers are few. Ask the Lord of the harvest, therefore, to send out workers into his harvest field.' "

Luke 10:2

We need more feeling for the field. "They are ripe for harvest." It is important to work for the Lord, as well as worship Him.

———————————

" 'For whoever wants to save his life will lose it, but whoever loses his life for me will save it.' "

Luke 9:24

There is no gift like the gift of thyself. The only thing that we save is what we give away. Lose yourself in the work of Christ here, and you will find yourself in Heaven.

———————————

" '. . . anyone who gives you a cup of water in my name because you belong to Christ will certainly not lose his reward.' "

Mark 9:41

Our attitude toward the little things is important.

———————————

"Do not withhold good from those who deserve it, when it is in your power to act."
Proverbs 3:27

If you are a Christian, the best thing that you can do for your neighbors is to introduce them to your best friend, Jesus. "He who wins souls is wise."

———————

"So this weak brother, for whom Christ died, is destroyed by your knowledge."
1 Corinthians 8:11

The man who helps another finds his way is on the right track himself. "Keep on loving each other as brothers."

———————

"That if you confess with your mouth, 'Jesus is Lord,' and believe in your heart that God raised him from the dead, you will be saved."
Romans 10:9

The Christian life ought to be full of believing, telling and sharing.

———————

"He said to them, 'Go into all the world and preach the good news to all creation. Whoever believes and is baptized will be saved, but whoever does not believe will be condemned.' "

Mark 16:15, 16

The gospel is a subpoena, and every Christian is obligated to go out and serve it on a lost world. **"And surely I am with you."**

———————

"My tongue will tell of your righteous acts all day long . . ."

Psalm 71:24

Every Christian ought to have a testimony and not be ashamed to tell it.

———————

"For we cannot help speaking about what we have seen and heard."

Acts 4:20

The man who has met the Lord is bound to tell of the meeting. **"Let the redeemed of the Lord say this — those he redeemed from the hand of the foe."**

———————

". . . he who wins souls is wise."

Proverbs 11:30

The best time that a man spends on earth is what he does in the interest of Heaven.

———————————

" 'Come, follow me,' Jesus said, 'and I will make you fishers of men.' "

Mark 1:17

If it has not been your happy privilege to point a soul to Christ, it matters little else what your achievements have been. There is no business like God's business.

———————————

"For I have not hesitated to proclaim to you the whole will of God."

Acts 20:27

The world has heard too much of the gospel according to man and too little of the Gospel according to God. Man is at his best when he is telling what the Lord has to say. "Preach the Word."

———————————

"Who gave himself for us to redeem us from all wickedness and to purify for himself a people that are his very own, eager to do what is good."

Titus 2:14

God is looking for bold and busy people to do big things.

―――――――――

". . . Be faithful, even to the point of death, and I will give you the crown of life."

Revelation 2:10

Be a career Christian.

―――――――――

". . . Here am I. Send me!"

Isaiah 6:8

The greatest contribution is the gift of ourselves in the service of the Lord. A lot of big jobs are waiting to be filled by dedicated little people.

―――――――――

"Those who are wise will shine like the brightness of the heavens, and those who lead many to righteousness, like the stars for ever and ever."

Daniel 12:3

Do something lasting and leave something lasting. Major in the main things of life; all else will vanish.

———————

"Now get up and go into the city, and you will be told what you must do."

Acts 9:6

God will take the willing worker, all-out for Christ, in preference to the wise ones who feel they have all the answers.

———————

The Sovereignty of God....

The Sovereignty of God

"The earth is the Lord's, and everything in it, the world, and all who live in it."

Psalm 24:1

Once the ownership is established, we shouldn't have any trouble with obedience. "You are not your own." We have been purchased not with gold or silver, but by the precious blood of Christ.

" 'Has not my hand made all these things?' "

Acts 7:50

So little of our lives revolve around Him, who created us, and the world that we live in. So much depends on our attitude toward Him and what we do with the Saviour.

" 'Do not turn to idols or make gods of cast metal for yourselves. I am the Lord your God.' "

Leviticus 19:4

Anything that is put ahead of God will be left behind. "You shall worship the Lord your God and him only will you serve."

"For from him and through him and to him are all things. To him be the glory forever! Amen."

Romans 11:36

Life was made to revolve around God, and when it doesn't, we run into reverses.

" 'Ah, Sovereign Lord, you have made the heavens and the earth by your great power and outstretched arm. Nothing is too hard for you.' "

Jeremiah 32:17

God can do anything, and without Him, we can do nothing.

"For by him all things were created: things in heaven and on earth, visible and invisible, whether thrones or powers or rulers or authorities; all things were created by him and for him."

Colossians 1:16, 17

God has a copyright on all creations. Man merely makes the discovery that after all is said and done, he belongs to Him.

"The earth is the Lord's, and everything in it, the world, and all who live in it."

Psalm 24:1

This just about settles it for God. Happy is the man who recognizes who holds the whole world in the palm of His hand.

———————

" '. . . they will know that I am the Lord.' "

Ezekiel 38:23

God has a way of making Himself known and heard. "Seek the Lord while he may be found; call on him while he is near."

———————

" 'As the heavens are higher than the earth, so are my ways higher than your ways and my thoughts than your thoughts.' "

Isaiah 55:9

This does not mean that God is out of reach, but only that many times His reasoning is different from ours. Don't spend a lot of time trying to figure God out; just release your faith in humble obedience to His will and way.

———————

". . . the Lord, who does these things that have been known for ages."

Acts 15:17, 18

Never mind if we can't figure everything out, so long as we know that our faithful Creator has everything in control. "Underneath are the everlasting arms." "Trust and obey."

"Then the Lord said to Moses, 'Get up early in the morning, confront Pharaoh and say to him, "This is what the Lord, the God of the Hebrews, says: Let my people go, so that they may worship me, or this time I will send the full force of my plagues against you and against your officials and your people, so you may know that there is no one like me in all the earth." ' "

Exodus 9:13, 14

The Lord has a way of getting the attention of those who are aggravating His people . . . and no one will doubt that He has spoken.

"Don't you know that you yourselves are God's temple and that God's Spirit lives in you? If anyone destroys God's temple, God will destroy him; for God's temple is sacred, and you are that temple."

1 Corinthians 3:16, 17

Man is the property of God and He will not forever tolerate trespassing.

———————————

"Now to him who is able to do immeasurably more than all we ask or imagine, according to his power that is at work within us."

Ephesians 3:20

No one can look at this and limit God. "For nothing is impossible with God." "I am the Lord, the God of all mankind. Is anything too hard for me?"

———————————

" 'Do not turn to idols or make gods of cast metal for yourselves. I am the Lord your God.' "

Leviticus 19:4

Anything that is put ahead of God will be left behind. "You shall worship the Lord your God and Him only shall you serve." Attend the services in your church and pray for God's servant. Blessings will be yours.

———————

"Come, let us bow down in worship, let us kneel before the Lord our Maker."

Psalm 95:6

Worship is more than sound. It is an act! It is a bowing of our wills and ways, a surrender to Him. We must not make the mistake of worshipping a cause, another Christian or even the Church. All the glory is due to God and must go to Him. Praise Him!

———————

"Let all the earth fear the Lord; let all the people of the world revere him."

Psalm 33:8

We need but to look around us to know that there is a greater power above us. The need of the hour is for the created to have more respect for the Creator.

———————

"Know that the Lord is God. It is he who made us, and we are his; we are his people, the sheep of his pasture."

Psalm 100:3

The strain of life and the sting of death are removed when we come to sit at the feet of the dear Shepherd. Jesus said, "I am the good shepherd. The good shepherd lays down his life for the sheep."

———————

" 'Can anyone hide in secret places so that I cannot see him?' declares the Lord. 'Do not I fill heaven and earth?' declares the Lord."

Jeremiah 23:24

God is everywhere, all powerful, and He loves you. Come out of your hiding, wherever you are, and open yourself up to His tender touch. Your Heavenly Father will forgive you. Whom the Son sets free is free indeed.

———————

" 'I am the Lord; that is my name! I will not give my glory to another or my praise to idols.' "

Isaiah 42:8

Love and appreciate others and even love yourself, but all the glory and the praise, plus the greatest of our love must go to Him. All that we are, have, or will be is because of Him. "He hath made us and not we ourselves." Oh God, our Heavenly Father, we praise You and give honor and glory to Your name. Thank You for Jesus and the Holy Spirit and Your Word. We praise You for abundant life here and eternal life in Heaven, through Jesus Christ, Your Son. Amen.

"On that day the Lord will shield those who live in Jerusalem, so that the feeblest among them will be like David, and the house of David will be like God, like the Angel of the Lord going before them."

Zechariah 12:8

With God, the weakest of vessels takes on the power and the authority of the Lord. "I am with you and will rescue you."

"The Lord will be king over the whole earth. On that day there will be one Lord, and his name the only name."

Zechariah 14:9

The day will come when the One who made it all will rule over all. Blessed are those subjects who will already have made Him Lord of Lords and King of Kings.

———————

"All the ends of the earth will remember and turn to the Lord, and all the families of the nations will bow down before him, for dominion belongs to the Lord and he rules over the nations."

Psalm 22:27, 28

God has His way of bringing to pass what He has said. Woe to the people and nations that get in the way.

———————

" 'You heavens above, rain down righteousness; let the clouds shower it down. Let the earth open wide, let salvation spring up, let righteousness grow with it; I, the Lord, have created it.' "

Isaiah 45:8

Listen to the Lord! A God who can speak with authority like that certainly has a good word for you. "Ask and it will be given to you; seek and you will find; knock and the door will be opened to you." Praise God.

"Be still, and know that I am God; I will be exalted among the nations, I will be exalted in the earth."

Psalm 46:10

Some of the greatest victories that you will ever experience will not be in working for God, but in waiting on Him. Come out of your struggles and into His stillness and "know Him."

"The God of peace will soon crush Satan under your feet. The grace of our Lord Jesus be with you."

Romans 16:20

Keep this in mind no matter how things look. God is in charge. Father, help us to recognize Your ability and our authority as believers. In Jesus' name. Amen.

"Jesus looked at them and said, 'With man this is impossible, but not with God; all things are possible with God.' "

Mark 10:27

Nothing is out of reach as long as we can reach our Heavenly Father, and we can. Jesus said, "I am the way." Let's go with Him.

———————

"So then, no more boasting about men! All things are yours."

1 Corinthians 3:21

Look at all we miss by not looking to God. "And my God will meet all your needs according to his glorious riches in Christ Jesus."

———————

Spiritual Birth....

Spiritual Birth

"Therefore, if anyone is in Christ, he is a new creation; the old has gone, the new has come!"

2 Corinthians 5:17

Our meeting with Christ always makes the difference. We will know it, and so will others. "Let your light shine before men, that they may see your good deeds and praise your Father in heaven."

"Therefore, there is now no condemnation for those who are in Christ Jesus."

Romans 8:1

Regeneration in Christ brings release. Refuse to live in the past. "If anyone is in Christ, he is a new creation; the old has gone, the new has come!"

"In reply Jesus declared, 'I tell you the truth, no one can see the kingdom of God unless he is born again.' "

John 3:3

The new birth is a lot more than a decision to do a little better. It is a departure of the old nature, giving way to new life in Christ. It becomes "Christ in you, the hope of glory." Father, help us all to see how easy it is to receive Jesus, and yet how easy it is to pass Him by and lose eternal life forever."

"But now you must rid yourselves of all such things as these: anger, rage, malice, slander, and filthy language from your lips. Do not lie to each other . . ."

Colossians 3:8, 9

Here are some things that we can do without in this life. When we put on the new man through Christ, then we can put off the old man with all his evil deeds.

"I will give you a new heart and put a new spirit in you . . ."

Ezekiel 36:26

You can't whitewash the old heart and expect a new spirit. Allow God to make the exchange of a lifetime, and give you a new heart and a new spirit for a new year. "The old is gone, the new has come!"

". . . I am making everything new!"

Revelation 21:5

God has the power and is willing to give us a new start. If you are tired of the old life, then accept the new one that He has for you. "If anyone is in Christ, he is a new creation; the old has gone, the new has come!"

"In reply Jesus declared, 'I tell you the truth, no one can see the kingdom of God unless he is born again.' "

John 3:3

Never have there been so many churches with the evidence of so few real Christians. It is highly possible for one to be known by everyone in church and yet be a stranger to Christ.

"The voice spoke from heaven a second time, 'Do not call anything impure that God has made clean.' "

Acts 11:9

Whatever and whomever God touches is never the same. Regeneration elevates. "If anyone is in Christ, he is a new creation; the old has gone, the new has come!"

———————

"In reply Jesus declared, 'I tell you the truth, no one can see the kingdom of God unless he is born again.' "

John 3:3

What the world needs is not only born leaders, but born-again leaders. You can be born again. "You must be born again."

———————

"In reply Jesus declared, 'I tell you the truth, no one can see the kingdom of God unless he is born again.' "

John 3:3

What good would it do to refine man if he is not regenerated? The heart of man, as well as the head of man, must be reached. Culture may polish up a man, but only Christ can really cleanse him.

———————

" 'Come now, let us reason together.' says the Lord. 'Though your sins are like scarlet, they shall be as white as snow; though they are red as crimson, they shall be like wool.' "

Isaiah 1:18

If an artist is able to take a piece of junk and make it into a thing of beauty, think of what the Lord can do with our lives turned over to Him. Let the Lord Redeemer recycle your life today. You will be glad with the results.

———————

"In reply Jesus declared, 'I tell you the truth, no one can see the kingdom of God unless he is born again.' "

John 3:3

Do you know the process? Simply pray, Father, I receive Jesus as my Saviour on the basis that He died for my sins, and that I cannot be saved without Him. I repent of my sins, and I release it all to You. In Jesus' name. Amen. Thank You.

———————

" 'Flesh gives birth to flesh, but the Spirit gives birth to spirit.' "

John 3:6

Here is the heart of God in the interest of the souls of men. The next move is yours. Jesus said, "Come to me, and whoever comes to me I will never drive away."

———————————

"In reply Jesus declared, 'I tell you the truth, no one can see the kingdom of God unless he is born again.'" *John 3:3*

This is more than a term. It is an experience, without which, we are not ready to meet God. It means being born from above, and it can happen right now by praying a prayer like this. Father, I repent of my sins, and I receive the Lord Jesus, Your Son, into my heart as my personal Savior and Lord of my life. Amen.

———————————

"'Enter through the narrow gate. For wide is the gate and broad is the road that leads to destruction, and many enter through it. But small is the gate and narrow the road that leads to life, and only a few find it.'"

Matthew 7:13, 14

Heaven is no walk-in or pushover. "No one can see the kingdom of God unless he is born again."

"To him who is able to keep you from falling and to present you before his glorious presence without fault and with great joy."

Jude 24

Don't worry about the carry-over of the old life once you have surrendered it to Him. "If any one is in Christ, he is a new creation." "I am making everything new!"

"For the Lord himself will come down from heaven, with a loud command, with the voice of the archangel and with the trumpet call of God, and the dead in Christ will rise first. After that, we who are still alive and are left will be caught up together with them in the clouds to meet the Lord in the air. And so we will be with the Lord forever."

1 Thessalonians 4:16, 17

What a beautiful picture of the future! But remember, there is no reunion without regeneration! "No one can see the kingdom of God unless he is born again." You can take care of that in the next moment by turning from your sins and inviting Jesus into your heart.

———————————

Spiritual Neglect....

Spiritual Neglect

"Yet I hold this against you: You have forsaken your first love."

Revelation 2:4

The Lord's message to the Church is simply to "come back" from our wanderings, get off the religious routine bit, and get on with the message that man is a sinner and Jesus is the Saviour, and without Him there is no redemption. Only in this is there hope for the Church and help for the world.

———————

"For although they knew God, they neither glorified him as God nor gave thanks to him, but their thinking became futile and their foolish hearts were darkened. Although they claimed to be wise, they became fools."

Romans 1:21, 22

The road to decay is often marked by signs of deceit, ingratitude, self-esteem and God rejection.

———————

"Then Peter remembered the word Jesus had spoken: 'Before the rooster crows, you will disown me three times.' And he went outside and wept bitterly."

Matthew 26:75

Tears have been the way back for many discouraged Christians who have warmed themselves by the enemy's fire. He will not turn thee away.

"Yet I hold this against you: You have forsaken your first love."

Revelation 2:4

It is a costly thing to allow cares and circumstances to crowd Christ out of your life. "Return."

"It is for freedom that Christ has set us free. Stand firm, then, and do not let yourselves be burdened again by a yoke of slavery."

Galatians 5:1

We must enjoy and exercise the freedom that Christ has given us, or become subject to the former things that bound us.

"Like a city whose walls are broken down is a man who lacks self-control."

Proverbs 25:28

It is so easy to lose control if Christ is not at the center of your life. "Let the Spirit of Christ reign in your heart."

———————————

" 'Because of the increase of wickedness, the love of most will grow cold.' "

Matthew 24:12

One of the great signs of the times is the priority given to sin. "As it was in the days of Noah, so it will be at the coming of the Son of Man."

———————————

"For the love of money is a root of all kinds of evil. Some people, eager for money, have wandered from the faith and pierced themselves with many griefs."

1 Timothy 6:10

If you are inclined to be impressed by those who appear to have it made, take another look at what it has made of them.

"Seek first his kingdom and his righteousness, and all these things will be given to you as well."

"If they have escaped the corruption of the world by knowing our Lord and Savior Jesus Christ and are again entangled in it and overcome, they are worse off at the end than they were at the beginning."

2 Peter 2:20

In a world of pollution talk, it makes good sense for us to hear what the Lord has to say about the future a man has who cleans the air regarding his spiritual experience, and then sets out on a "do it yourself" plan. Beware, lest we ignore the pitfalls and disregard the power of Him who is able to keep us. Remember, the Lord, Jesus said, "Apart from me you can do nothing." . . . but we are more than conquerors through Him that loved us.

"It is for freedom that Christ has set us free. Stand firm, then, and do not let yourselves be burdened again by a yoke of slavery."

Galatians 5:1

Most of our fears are of our own making, because we have not made Him Master and Lord of our life. "Perfect love drives out fear." "Fear not for I am with you . . ."

———————

"But the people said to Joshua, 'No! We will serve the Lord.' "

Joshua 24:21

How many of us have made the same commitment to the Lord, only to lose it in a shuffle of simple things we regarded as important? This week, take your family back to the House of God and get the same good feeling that only a renewal of your faith can bring. You need your church and your church needs you.

———————

"But they soon forgot what he had done and did not wait for his counsel. So he gave them what they asked for, but sent a wasting disease upon them."

Psalm 106:13, 15

Many a person has discovered that what they begged God for satisfied the flesh for a season, but it starved the soul. "Seek first his kingdom and his righteousness, and all these things will be given to you as well."

"Then Moses went up to God, and the Lord called to him from the mountain and said, 'This is what you are to say to the house of Jacob and what you are to tell the people of Israel . . . "Now if you obey me fully and keep my covenant, then out of all nations you will be my treasured possession." ' "

Exodus 19:3, 5

If the fulfillment of His promises seems to elude us, it could be that we have failed to obey the conditions.

"Now then, stand here, because I am going to confront you with evidence before the Lord as to all the righteous acts performed by the Lord for you and your fathers."

1 Samuel 12:7

In a fast moving world, there is a great danger of forgetting where we are going and where we started. Stand still and see the salvation of the Lord.

". . . Today, if you hear his voice, do not harden your hearts . . ."

Hebrews 3:15

The man who ignores the voice of God runs the risk of never hearing it again. "My Spirit will not contend with man forever . . ."

———————

"My Spirit will not contend with man forever . . ."

Genesis 6:3

Pity the person who, through his own neglect, puts himself out of the reach of God. The Lord has sent the Holy Spirit to bring you in. Don't turn Him away.

———————

"Do not neglect your gift . . ."

1 Timothy 4:14

We need to develop our own God-given talents, instead of trying to duplicate what He has given to another.

———————

"How shall we escape if we ignore such a great salvation? . . ."

Hebrews 2:3

Put-off and put-on are two of man's greatest enemies. Give God your answer today to this great question. "My Spirit will not contend with man forever."

"Jesus replied, 'No one who puts his hand to the plow and looks back is fit for service in the kingdom of God.' "

Luke 9:62

More Christians are needed with the forward look. Too much time is spent at the tombstones of past experiences.

"I will heal their waywardness and love them freely, for my anger has turned away from them."

Hosea 14:4

Every man knows where he is with God, but nothing happens until he turns around. "I have considered my ways and have turned." "Unless you repent, you too will all perish."

Trusting God....

Trusting God

"Praise be to the Lord, who has given rest to his people Israel just as he promised. Not one word has failed of all the good promises he gave through his servant Moses."

1 Kings 8:56

Look at the record and leave the rest to Him. He will keep His Word with you. We are but to claim it.

———————————

"But Joseph said to them, 'Don't be afraid. Am I in the place of God? You intended to harm me, but God intended it for good to accomplish what is now being done, the saving of many lives. So then, don't be afraid. I will provide for you and your children.' And he reassured them and spoke kindly to them."

Genesis 50:19, 20

God has a way of taking what seems to be a big mistake and making a great miracle out of it. As for us, we are inclined to get disappointments and appointments mixed up. Walk away from your problem and let God work on the answer. When you see what He comes up with, you will be glad you didn't try to work it out.

———————————

"So that your trust may be in the Lord, I teach you today, even you. Have I not written thirty sayings for you, sayings of counsel and knowledge."

Proverbs 22:19, 20

Life's answers are lost to us because we keep leaning on our own understanding or taking the advice of those who are as much in the dark as we are. Read the Bible every day and apply it to your everyday need.

". . . you have made the heavens and the earth by your great power and outstretched arm. Nothing is too hard for you."

Jeremiah 32:17

If He can make the heaven and the earth, you surely can trust Him with your problem. Believe that. He is great enough and willing to meet your every need. "All authority in heaven and on earth has been given to me."

"Trust in the Lord forever, for the Lord, the Lord, is the Rock eternal."

Isaiah 26:4

Enlist your life in the service of the Lord forever. Don't worry about the "holding out," for in Him is everlasting strength. "I will uphold you with my righteous right hand." Have faith in God.

"And without faith it is impossible to please God, because anyone who comes to him must believe that he exists and that he rewards those who earnestly seek him."

Hebrews 11:6

Nothing that we can do for God can ever take the place of our trust in Him. It is altogether possible to be a tireless worker for the Lord and, yet, to be timid in our trust.

"To you, O Lord, I lift up my soul; in you I trust, O my God."

Psalm 25:1, 2

The man who lifts the burdens of life to God in sincerity will never be let down. "He cares for you."

"This is what the Lord says — your Redeemer, the Holy One of Israel: 'I am the Lord your God, who teaches you what is best for you, who directs you in the way you should go.' "

Isaiah 48:17

Don't hesitate to ask God for guidance. Don't question the way He leads. He will guide you into all truth.

"But as for me, it is good to be near God. I have made the Sovereign Lord my refuge; I will tell of all your deeds."

Psalm 73:28

Our greatest need is to be near to God. All else that is good and worthwhile will follow. "Come near to God, and he will come near to you."

"Jesus looked at them and said, 'With man this is impossible, but not with God; all things are possible with God.' "

Mark 10:27

You have tried everything else, why not try God? He is able to do and undo, and is limited only by what we will believe Him for. "I the Lord do not change."

" 'It is easier for heaven and earth to disappear than for the least stroke of a pen to drop out of the Law.' "

Luke 16:17

The Lord has never been known to go back on His Word or back down on His promises. "Only believe."

"When I am afraid, I will trust in you."

Psalm 56:3

If fear overtakes you, hurry to your Heavenly Father. He loves you and has the answer for every problem.

"I will not violate my covenant or alter what my lips have uttered."

Psalm 89:34

In an age of broken promises, God stands ready to keep His Word with the humblest believer.

————————

"When I am afraid, I will trust in you."
Psalm 56:3

When we treat fear with trust, all the terrors of life must go. "Never will I leave you; never will I forsake you."

————————

"See, I am doing a new thing! Now it springs up; do you not perceive it? I am making a way in the desert and streams in the wasteland."
Isaiah 43:19

We serve a creative God whose power adjusts to every problem of life. He will walk you through your wilderness, making a way where there is no way. Trust Him.

————————

"The Lord helps them and delivers them; he delivers them from the wicked and saves them, because they take refuge in him."
Psalm 37:40

The Lord is in the deliverance business. Special delivery! "I am the Lord, the God of all mankind. Is anything too hard for me?"

_____

Words of Warning....

Words of Warning

" 'What good is it for a man to gain the whole world, yet forfeit his soul? Or what can a man give in exchange for his soul?' "

Mark 8:36, 37

An eternity without God and the good things He has prepared is a terrible price to pay for having our own way over things that will soon pass away. "But seek first his kingdom and his righteousness, and all these things will be given to you as well."

"God is a righteous judge, a God who expresses his wrath every day."

Psalm 7:11

He is a God of love, compassion, and long-suffering, but He is also a God of judgment. You cannot forever trample under foot the Word of God, the stern commandments of God, reject His Son, and go unpunished.

" 'So you also must be ready, because the Son of Man will come at an hour when you do not expect him.' "

Matthew 24:44

A person who is not ready to die is not ready to live. A person who is not ready to meet his Master in His second coming cannot fully appreciate the fact that He came the first time.

"You shall not misuse the name of the Lord your God."

Deuteronomy 5:11

Think on the holiness of God. Dwell on the power He has over the world and you, and let the mind of the Master be the master of your mind. Remember, "Surely the arm of the Lord is not too short to save, nor his ear too dull to hear."

"Just as man is destined to die once, and after that to face judgment."

Hebrews 9:27

That we must appear to account for the way we have lived this life is a truth that we must all face. How we live and how we die will determine our eternal future.

" 'You will look for me, but you will not find me; and where I am, you cannot come.' "

John 7:34

Man pays a terrible price for his pride. "Today, if you hear his voice, do not harden your hearts."

" 'Behold, I am coming soon! My reward is with me, and I will give to everyone according to what he has done.' "

Revelation 22:12

The world's greatest surprise may be at our doorstep. He has not said in vain, "I shall come again." Even so, come Lord Jesus.

" 'But they paid no attention . . .' "

Matthew 22:5

Humanity has ever been the same. The seriousness of the invitation did not register with them then, and the majority of our day do not see the tragedy of their refusal in accepting the Saviour. Decide now. A man may be almost saved, yet entirely lost. Don't make light of the invitation. Eternity is a long time to remember that you rejected it.

———————

" 'What good will it be for a man if he gains the whole world, yet forfeits his soul? Or what can a man give in exchange for his soul?' "

Matthew 16:26

Nothing on earth is worth keeping you out of Heaven. Count the cost!

———————

"Be careful that you do not forget the Lord your God, failing to observe his commands, his laws and his decrees that I am giving you this day."

Deuteronomy 8:11

The man or the nation who forgets God will be reminded. Keep God in mind and His work at heart.

———————

" 'I tell you, on that night two people will be in one bed; one will be taken and the other left. Two women will be grinding grain together; one will be taken and the other left.' "

Luke 17:34, 35

Will you be among the missing or the misinformed? Read your Bible. Jesus said, "I will come again."

"Jesus said, 'I am with you for only a short time, and then I go to the one who sent me. You will look for me, but you will not find me; and where I am, you cannot come.' "

John 7:33, 34

Jesus is saying: "You will look for me, but you will not find me." "My spirit will not contend with man forever." "Seek the Lord while he may be found; call on him while he is near."

"He gave you manna to eat in the desert, something your fathers had never known, to humble and to test you so that in the end it might go well with you."

Deuteronomy 8:16

If you have moved on to bigger things, as you see it, you would be wise to remember who took care of you in the wilderness. Otherwise, you may have another look at it!

"Then he said to them: 'Nation will rise against nation, and kingdom against kingdom. There will be great earthquakes, famines and pestilences in various places, and fearful events and great signs from heaven.' "

Luke 21:10, 11

More signs that His coming could be soon. When you read the Bible today, you would think that it was written yesterday. Jesus said, "The Son of Man will come at an hour when you do not expect him."

"Do not worship any other god, for the Lord, whose name is Jealous, is a jealous God."

Exodus 34:14

Look out for the little gods. They have a way of growing, and no matter how small, they can separate us from the true and living God.

"Be careful that you do not forget the Lord your God, failing to observe his commands, his laws and his decrees that I am giving you this day."

Deuteronomy 8:11

Don't forget to remember from whence you came, and who has brought you to where you are, and where you are going.

––––––––––––––

" 'I tell you, on that night two people will be in one bed; one will be taken and the other left. Two women will be grinding grain together; one will be taken and the other left.'

'Where Lord?' they asked.

He replied, 'Where there is a dead body, there the vultures will gather.' "

Luke 17:34-37

Here is a picture of the final day on earth of people who will probably have plans of what all they are going to do for the Lord, and others who were going to get right with the Lord. Do it now. "You do not know the day or the hour."

––––––––––––––

". . . there will be a resurrection of both the righteous and the wicked."

Acts 24:15

Make no mistake about it. We all must appear before our Maker. You may have all the answers now, but how will it be when you stand before Him? Live today as though tomorrow you would face Him.

———————

" '. . . How is it that you don't know how to interpret this present time?' "

Luke 12:56

If we fail to heed the signs, we will soon lose our way. These are days of signs and wonders, the greatest wonder being that we fail to see it.

———————

" 'Men of Galilee,' they said, 'why do you stand here looking into the sky? This same Jesus, who has been taken from you into heaven, will come back in the same way you have seen him go into heaven.' "

Acts 1:11

The greatest surprise this world has ever known could be just around the corner. "You do not know the day or the hour." Jesus said, "I will come again."

———————

" 'But the one who does not know and does things deserving punishment will be beaten with few blows. From everyone who has been given much, much will be demanded; and from the one who has been entrusted with much, much more will be asked.' "

Luke 12:48

God will require of nations and individuals a final accounting of what we did with what He gave us.

" 'For God so loved the world that he gave his one and only Son, that whoever believes in him shall not perish but have eternal life.' "

John 3:16

Here in the Word of God is the world's greatest news coupled with the saddest news. The future of every person is dependent on whether he ignores it or embraces it.

"Though you already know all this, I want to remind you that the Lord delivered his people out of Egypt, but later destroyed those who did not believe."

Jude 5

Don't presume on the patience of the longsuffering Lord. "My spirit will not contend with man forever."

"First of all, you must understand that in the last days scoffers will come, scoffing and following their own evil desires. They will say, 'Where is this "coming" he promised? Ever since our fathers died, everything goes on as it has since the beginning of creation.' "

2 Peter 3:3, 4

This is the day of the vocal unbelievers. The day of victory and vengeance of the Lord cannot be far away. Behold, He cometh. When ye shall see these things come to pass, look up.

"If anyone's name was not found written in the book of life, he was thrown into the lake of fire."

Revelation 20:15

For the man who is trying to make a name here, it is good to give some serious thought as to where it will appear in the life to come.

———————

"Blow the trumpet in Zion; sound the alarm on my holy hill. Let all who live in the land tremble, for the day of the Lord is coming. It is close at hand."

Joel 2:1

It is the responsibility of every believer to sound the alarm. It is up to every man, on his own, to get up and answer the call. Don't turn the alarm off and go back to sleep, or let it run down. "My spirit will not contend with man forever."

———————

"Therefore this is what I will do to you, Israel, and because I will do this to you, prepare to meet your God, O Israel."

Amos 4:12

The most sobering thought in this life is that in the next we must account to Him who has made it. Where will you spend eternity? How are you spending life here?

"Do not be deceived: God cannot be mocked. A man reaps what he sows."

Galatians 6:7

A person has to be careful of the seed that he sows. The day of harvest will come.

"And if anyone takes words away from this book of prophecy, God will take away from him his share in the tree of life and in the holy city, which are described in this book."

Revelation 22:19

People who alter the Word to their liking will have to give an account to the Lord.

"And I saw the dead, great and small, standing before the throne, and books were opened. Another book was opened, which is the book of life. The dead were judged according to what they had done as recorded in the books."

Revelation 20:12

Never forget that we are judged by our works, but saved by His grace; and we must accept him as Saviour or face Him as Judge.

"The Lord has done what he predicted through me. The Lord has torn the kingdom out of your hands and given it to one of your neighbors — to David. Because you did not obey the Lord or carry out his fierce wrath against the Amalekites, the Lord has done this to you today."

1 Samuel 28:17, 18

Any time we get too busy to listen or too big to obey, the Lord always has someone waiting to take our place.

" 'I will turn your towns into ruins and you will be desolate. Then you will know that I am the Lord.

" 'Because you harbored an ancient hostility and delivered the Israelites over to the sword at the time of their calamity, the time their punishment reached its climax.' "

Ezekiel 35:4, 5

All mankind must remember that God cannot be pushed too far. He who is capable of great love is also capable of sure punishment.

"They provoked the Lord to anger by their wicked deeds, and a plague broke out among them."

Psalm 106:29

Perhaps we have yet to see the final cost of many of our achievements and the misuse of the great knowledge that God has entrusted to us.

" 'In hell, where he was in torment, he looked up and saw Abraham far away, and Lazarus by his side.' "

Luke 16:23

One minute after you have missed Heaven, you will know that hell is no myth. The only way out is in Him. "Believe in the Lord Jesus, and you will be saved."

"You shall not misuse the name of the Lord your God, for the Lord will not hold anyone guiltless who misuses his name."

Exodus 20:7

God is not taking lightly the language used involving His name and bringing reproach to His cause.

" 'Will your courage endure or your hands be strong in the day I deal with you? I the Lord have spoken, and I will do it.' "

Ezekiel 22:14

The judgment of God is no joke! Any nation or anyone who backs themselves into a corner, through open rebellion and unbelief, has good cause to be concerned. Jesus said, "Unless you repent, you too will all perish."

" 'Therefore keep watch, because you do not know the day or the hour.' "

Matthew 25:13

We are told not to set the time, but to make use of what we have left. In such an hour as ye think not, the Son of Man cometh. "Even so, come Lord Jesus."

" 'Nation will rise against nation, and kingdom against kingdom. There will be earthquakes in various places, and famines. These are the beginning of birth pains.' "

Mark 13:8

If you have missed the news, catch it in the Bible. You will probably be out in front! Thy Word is truth.

" 'Be on guard! Be alert! You do not know when that time will come.' "

Mark 13:33

Time is in God's hands. Talents are in our hands. We ought to use them wisely before time runs out. The time is short.

"Now the earth was corrupt in God's sight and was full of violence. So God said to Noah, 'I am going to put an end to all people, for the earth is filled with violence because of them. I am surely going to destroy both them and the earth.' "

Genesis 6:11, 13

God warns from the past what we can expect in the future. What they saw in the beginning, we are experiencing in the present. But look up and get ready. As it was in the days of Noah, so shall it be also in the days of the coming of the Son of Man.

" 'You also must be ready, because the Son of Man will come at an hour when you do not expect him.' "

Luke 12:40

When we least expect Him, Jesus Christ, unannounced, will come back to take away every believer. If it happened tonight, where would you be tomorrow?

"The eyes of the Lord are everywhere, keeping watch on the wicked and the good."

Proverbs 15:3

The Lord sees everything and knows every thought. No evil thing will go unnoticed. No good thing will go unrewarded.

"But suppose the servant says to himself, 'My master is taking a long time in coming.' . . . The master of that servant will come on a day when he does not expect him and at an hour he is not aware of. He will cut him to pieces and assign him a place with the unbelievers."

Luke 12:45, 46

The second coming of Christ will be swift and sure, full of shocks and surprises. Perhaps some of the most surprised will be His servants.

" 'Whoever believes in the Son has eternal life, but whoever rejects the Son will not see life, for God's wrath remains on him.' "

John 3:36

Here is what Jesus had to say about man's future. Everything that really counts is riding on what we do with Christ.

" '. . . there will be weeping and gnashing of teeth.' "

Matthew 24:51

This is how Jesus described a future without God and apart from Heaven. "Choose for yourselves this day whom you will serve."

"Seek the Lord while he may be found; call on him while he is near."

Isaiah 55:6

The risk of tomorrow is too great to ignore the important issues of today. This is your day.

" 'You will look for me, but you will not find me . . .' "

John 7:34

The worst thing that can happen to a man is not for his prayers to go unanswered, but for his prayers not to be heard.

"And as for us, why do we endanger ourselves every hour?"

1 Corinthians 15:30

The person who won't stand up for Christ here won't stand a chance in Heaven. It is a risky thing to live in this world and ignore its Creator.

"Just as man is destined to die once, and after that to face judgment."

Hebrews 9:27

The most sobering thought of life is that after it is all over, we must give an account of every minute of it.

"For the wages of sin is death, but the gift of God is eternal life in Christ Jesus our Lord."
Romans 6:23

Everyone is paid by the master he serves. Life here is full of pay-backs. Eternity is full of play-backs with no take-backs.

———————————

Miscellany....

Miscellany

" 'For God so loved the world that he gave his one and only Son, that whoever believes in him shall not perish but have eternal life.' "

John 3:16

This is Jesus telling what it took to bring mankind back to His Maker. To accept Him is life eternal. To reject Him is separation forever. Could this be your favorite verse which you have often quoted, but never experienced?

" 'I will remain in the world no longer, but they are still in the world, and I am coming to you. Holy Father, protect them by the power of your name — the name you gave me — so that they may be one as we are one.' "

John 17:11

The greatest need of the Church today is to have an old-fashioned family reunion with Jesus at the head of the table!

"So is my word that goes out from my mouth: It will not return to me empty, but will accomplish what I desire and achieve the purpose for which I sent it."

Isaiah 55:11

If we want to be a part of a sure producer, we need to make sure that we are projecting His Word. Remember, it's His Word, not ours, that He has promised to bless.

———————

"But if from there you seek the Lord your God, you will find him if you look for him with all your heart and with all your soul."

Deuteronomy 4:29

Whoever you are, and whatever you are along the road of life, if you get serious with God, you are going to see things you never dreamed possible. "Seek the Lord while he may be found; call on him while he is near."

———————

" 'I am the vine; you are the branches. If a man remains in me and I in him, he will bear much fruit; apart from me you can do nothing.' "

John 15:5

Abiding in Him is even more productive than activity for Him. " 'Not by might, nor by power, but by my Spirit,' says the Lord Almighty."

———————

"For Christ did not send me to baptize, but to preach the gospel — not with words of human wisdom, lest the cross of Christ be emptied of its power. For the message of the cross is foolishness to those who are perishing, but to us who are being saved it is the power of God."
1 Corinthians 1:17, 18

The cross is where the sins of the whole world were paid for . . . but every person must acknowledge it was for him, before he can be pardoned. A simple prayer will see you through. Father, I admit my sins. I acknowledge Jesus as the One who died for them. I receive Him now as my Saviour. In His name. Amen.

"May the words of my mouth and the meditation of my heart be pleasing in your sight, O Lord, my Rock and my Redeemer."
Psalm 19:14

Not only what we talk about, but what we think about, is screened by the Lord. Is it acceptable to the Lord?

"After forty years had passed, an angel appeared to Moses in the flames of a burning bush in the desert near Mount Sinai."

Acts 7:30

God is still speaking through unusual means, and many times through unknown people, to get His message across.

───────────────

" 'I tell you the truth, anyone who has faith in me will do what I have been doing. He will do even greater things than these, because I am going to the Father. And I will do whatever you ask in my name, so that the Son may bring glory to the Father. You may ask me for anything in my name, and I will do it.' "

John 14:12-14

Release your faith with me, as we look to the Father. Jesus, I take You at Your Word and believe now that multitudes will be saved, believers filled with the Holy Spirit, others healed, and needs met in every part of their lives, in Your name and for the glory of God. Amen.

───────────────

"For the wages of sin is death, but the gift of God is eternal life in Christ Jesus our Lord."

Romans 6:23

Every day, the average man neglects and forsakes the Greatest Gift in his mad and desperate search for worldly goods.

"And in the church God has appointed first of all apostles, second prophets, third teachers, then workers of miracles, also those having gifts of healing, those able to help others, those with gifts of administration, and those speaking in different kinds of tongues."

1 Corinthians 12:28

The average church is without New Testament excitement, because we have regarded ourselves as engineers of a program, rather than instruments through which the Holy Spirit can demonstrate His power.

"Then the Lord said to Joshua, 'See, I have delivered Jericho into your hands, along with its king and its fighting men.' . . . and they took the city."

Joshua 6:2, 20

The Bible is full of stories about ordinary people who went to war armed with nothing but the Word of God and won. "The grass withers and the flowers fall, but the word of our God stands forever."

———————

" 'For where two or three come together in my name, there am I with them.' "

Matthew 18:20

Careful that you don't make light of a few believers gathered, unless you want to take the responsibility of counting the presence of the Saviour as nothing.

———————

"Surely the arm of the Lord is not too short to save, nor his ear too dull to hear."

Isaiah 59:1

God has a strong arm, a ready ear, and a compassionate heart . . . and He loves you. Right now you can get right with Him. Father, in the next moment, help the readers to take care of all eternity by receiving Jesus into their hearts. Amen.

———————

"But thanks be to God! He gives us the victory through our Lord Jesus Christ."

1 Corinthians 15:57

How true it is militarily or spiritually, there is no substitute for victory. Don't settle for a stand-off. "In all these things we are more than conquerors through him who loved us."

———————

"The fruit of righteousness will be peace; the effect of righteousness will be quietness and confidence forever."

Isaiah 32:17

When we see the good that righteous living offers here and in the hereafter, can we really consider anything else? "The way of transgressors is hard." "Righteousness exalts a nation, but sin is a disgrace to any people."

———————

"For what I received I passed on to you as of first importance: that Christ died for our sins according to the Scriptures."

1 Corinthians 15:3

The shame of our Christian experience is that we have missed the magnitude of the cross. Daily, we need to remember that He died in our place, for our sins, and that our pardon is only in believing it and receiving Him.

"You are my hiding place; you will protect me from trouble and surround me with songs of deliverance.   *Selab*"
Psalm 32:7

The only security that will stand up is in the shelter of His arms. Come out, come out, wherever you are, from your own hiding place of fear and fright into the haven of rest provided in the resurrected Christ, and go free forever.

"The heart is deceitful above all things and beyond cure . . ."
Jeremiah 17:9

The heart is what we are and where we live. It remains so until it is renovated and made ready for the Redeemer to move in. Give Him His rightful place in your heart.

"He gives strength to the weary and increases the power of the weak."

Isaiah 40:29

The Christian's true strength is realized only in his whole-hearted surrender. The way out is up.

––––––––––

" 'Even now the reaper draws his wages, even now he harvests the crop for eternal life, so that the sower and the reaper may be glad together.' "

John 4:36

Life is a matter of sowing and reaping. Be careful what you sow; the harvest will come with rejoicing or with regrets.

––––––––––

"Then the disciples went out and preached everywhere, and the Lord worked with them and confirmed his word by the signs that accompanied it."

Mark 16:20

The Christian life should be full of signs and wonders.

––––––––––

"But thanks be to God! He gives us the victory through our Lord Jesus Christ."

1 Corinthians 15:57

There is a victory in the valley with Him who gives us a passing gear and a rising gear. The Lord takes the pressure and struggle out of religion, and lets us know that there are good times in God's service. Too many of us are content in holding on to what we have, at the cost of overlooking what God has for us.

―――――――――

" 'Whoever does God's will is my brother and sister and mother.' "

Mark 3:35

The people close to Christ will be those who have chosen His will above theirs. "Your will be done."

―――――――――

" 'And whoever wants to be first must be slave of all.' "

Mark 10:44

Not many people are aspiring to the great position of a true servant to mankind and our Maker. Most of us become slaves to goals without God.

———————

"And my God will meet all your needs according to his glorious riches in Christ Jesus."

Philippians 4:19

Things will come a great deal easier in life, once we get our eyes off earthly circumstances and catch a glimpse of the Heavenly supply. "I and all I have are yours."

———————

"With your help I can advance against a troop; with my God I can scale a wall."

Psalm 18:29

Don't worry about the walls if you are moving in His Divine will. March against them in His name, and they will fall.

———————

"Go to the ant, you sluggard; consider its ways and be wise!"

Proverbs 6:6

God has placed a lot of little things on earth to teach us big lessons.

" 'Come to me, all you who are weary and burdened, and I will give you rest. For my yoke is easy and my burden is light. Take my yoke upon you and learn from me, for I am gentle and humble in heart, and you will find rest for your souls.' "

Matthew 11:28-30

There is no rest and assurance, until we stop and surrender our all to the Almighty.

" 'What good will it be for a man if he gains the whole world, yet forfeits his soul? Or what can a man give in exchange for his soul?' "

Matthew 16:26

Neither the believer nor the unbeliever would ever need any prompting, if, for just once, we could catch a glimpse of the value of one soul.

"The Lord saw how great man's wickedness on the earth had become, and that every inclination of the thoughts of his heart was only evil at the time."

Genesis 6:5

This was God's observation at the beginning and certainly a parable of the present. Christ is the cure!

———————

" 'I will repay you for the years the locusts have eaten — the great locust and the young locust, the other locusts and the locust swarm — my great army that I sent among you.' "

Joel 2:25

Some of man's hardest living is in the past. Don't worry about the wasted years. One good day with God will make up for it all. A day with the Lord is as a thousand years.

———————

" 'For the Son of Man came to seek and to save what was lost.' "

Luke 19:10

You have to get lost before you can be found. Self-sufficiency locks the Saviour out and makes a prisoner of the One who holds

the key. "Here I am! I stand at the door and knock."

"Who can discern his errors? Forgive my hidden faults."

Psalm 19:12

It is secret faults that keep us from Sacred thoughts. He, who is above all, knows what is underneath.

"Who can say, 'I have kept my heart pure; I am clean and without sin'?"

Proverbs 20:9

Can the rich, the poor, the educated, or the uneducated say it with authority? Can we, by our own goodness or deeds, make our hearts clean? No! Only through Christ can we have clean hearts and a good clean feeling between us and our fellow man.

"But he denied it. 'Woman, I don't know him,' he said."

Luke 22:57

If we expect Christ to stand up for us, we should speak out for Him. If we confess Him, He will also confess us before the Father and the Holy Angels.

"O land, land, land, hear the word of the Lord!"

Jeremiah 22:29

The need of our world is the same that it has ever been; more of God's Word, less of man's. "The word of the Lord stands forever."

"The Lord is my shepherd . . ."

Psalm 23:1

When the sheep get acquainted with the Shepherd, there is little else to worry about. "Submit to God and be at peace with him."

"Do not merely listen to the word, and so deceive yourselves. Do what it says."

James 1:22

Personal application is the intended purpose of the Scriptures, yet we are so busy applying them to others, that we forget that they are also a remedy for what ails us.

" 'Then they will go away to eternal punishment, but the righteous to eternal life.' "

Matthew 25:46

The crossroads of life extend all the way into eternity. "Choose for yourselves this day whom you will serve."

" 'And why do you worry about clothes? See how the lilies of the field grow. They do not labor or spin. Yet I tell you that not even Solomon in all his splendor was dressed like one of these.' "

Matthew 6:28, 29

God's Spirit shining from within gives the greatest outward beauty.

"The one who calls you is faithful and he will do it."

1 Thessalonians 5:24

Cheer up! God has His hand on you and is not going to leave you stranded. He who hath begun a good work in you will continue.

"The Lord came and stood there, calling as at the other times, 'Samuel! Samuel!'

Then Samuel said, 'Speak, for your servant is listening.' "

1 Samuel 3:10

Whether you are a child or an adult, stay open to the call of God. Who knows what all He may have in store for you. Father, call multitudes into Your service, today. In Jesus' name. Amen.

―――――――――

" 'Then you will know the truth, and the truth will set you free.' "

John 8:32

It is the truth that turns us around and sets us free. "Jesus answered, 'I am the way and the truth and the life. No one comes to the Father except through me.' " May this be the turning point and the liberation of multitudes in this moment, my Father, as they receive Your Son Jesus into their heart. In His name. Amen.

―――――――――

"For we brought nothing into the world, and we can take nothing out of it."

1 Timothy 6:7

Live only for the present, and you not only go out of this life empty-handed, but heavy-hearted. Make your life and means count for Christ.

———————

"God has made my heart faint . . ."
Job 23:16

The man who has a mellow spirit will be respected by his fellow man and used of the Lord.

———————

" 'I have come that they may have life, and have it to the full.' "
John 10:10

Many are still content to live on worldly scraps in preference to a Heavenly supply. Are you living above the clouds or in them?

———————

"Do not boast about tomorrow, for you do not know what a day may bring forth."
Proverbs 27:1

Many of our todays are spoiled by planning for tomorrows. "This is the day the Lord has made." Use it for His glory.

———————

" 'Those whom I love I rebuke and discipline. So be earnest, and repent.' "

Revelation 3:19

We must constantly be monitoring our motives, lest we project self above the Saviour and works above worship.

"Remember your Creator in the days of your youth . . ."

Ecclesiastes 12:1

You can't give God what's left of life and expect His best. Give Him the best and the rest of your life.

"Do not go about spreading slander among your people."

Leviticus 19:16

Some people can't remember a good deed and can't forget a bad one.

"I have no greater joy than to hear that my children are walking in the truth."

3 John 4

Honest talk is good, if it is followed by honest walk. Truth is a terror to the unrighteous and a test to the righteous.

———————

"And without faith it is impossible to please God, because anyone who comes to him must believe that he exists and that he rewards those who earnestly seek him."

Hebrews 11:6

———————

This speaks of more than a casual communication with the Lord. Do you have time for that? You need to make time!

———————

". . . The Lord is with you when you are with him. If you seek him, he will be found by you, but if you forsake him, he will forsake you."

2 Chronicles 15:2

———————

The Lord is not in hiding. He is as close as your call. Father, may multitudes meet You, today, in Jesus' name. Amen.

———————

"Do not merely listen to the word, and so deceive yourselves. Do what it says."

James 1:22

The Word of God is meant to be taken in and walked out. You will never relive today. Make it a good one with God's help.

———————

"The secret things belong to the Lord our God, but the things revealed belong to us and to our children forever, that we may follow all the words of this law."

Deuteronomy 29:29

Look at the open-door policy for all of His promises. Father, give us a bold faith to claim what You have provided. In Jesus' name. Amen.

———————

"Now to him who is able to do immeasurably more than all we ask or imagine, according to his power that is at work within us."

Ephesians 3:20

Release that power within you, and go on to victorious living. "The one who is in you is greater than the one who is in the world."

———————